To ⟨...⟩ ⟨...⟩,

May ⟨...⟩ aware ⟨...⟩ ⟨...⟩ follow through your every word thought + actions. —

Blessings of Guru Nanak.

⟨signature⟩ 6/12/17

GURMAT
Practical Self-Realisation

GURMAT

Practical Self-Realisation

Davinder Singh Panesar

DTF Publishers and Distributors
UK

GURMAT
Practical Self-Realisation
by
DAVINDER SINGH PANESAR

ISBN 978-1-901363-03-6

First Published June 2017

Price : £ 19.95

Publishers and Printed by :

DTF PUBLISHERS AND DISTRIBUTORS
117 Soho Road, Handsworth,
Birmingham, B21 9ST, UK
Tel: 0121 515 1183.

"Piya"

Contents

Chapter Four
Introducing Practises

Acknowledgements

"Piya"
The very act of seeking, transforms the seeker.

Through grace of Ik Akal Purekh, teachings of Guru Nanak, gurus, bhagats mystics and the linage of Kangaryian da baba Shaeed Singh Panesar, I have had the profound privilege to be born within a family with several enlightened, self-realized and self-sovereign individuals who practically demonstrated through their presence, practices and wisdom, the pinnacle of being human is divinity itself, expressed in their thought, speech and actions.

My heartfelt thanks to my mother, Mata Rattan Kaur, my esteemed and revered masters, Baba Ranjit Singh (UK), Brahmgyani Baba Arjun Singh ji (India), Baba Puran Singh ji (Kericho wale), Baba Puran Singh ji (UK), Professor Surindar Singh Kholi and Bhai Didar Singh Manku. I owe a great debt of thanks for the great academic thinkers in the fields of Sikh studies Professor Arvindpal Singh mandair and Dr Kamalroop Singh Birk who have worked, guided and helped me in my journey to knowing Sikhi and having the ability to translate, Gurmat concepts into mainstream dualistic western language. I would like to thank Professor Arvindpal Singh mandair taking the time and effort to edit this publication.

Without the tireless support, encouragement and motivation of my wife Shanta Kaur Panesar, my family Arjun, Amar, Harkrishan, Pritpal, Bob, Balbir, Bajinder, Dr Anupam Sanyal, and my dearest friends Tony and Jagdeep, (Qi

Rattan), Pushy, Jackie, Sonya, Neelu, Gurbinder Kalsi, Bob ham, Mata Pilar, Santa Maria, Medicina and all those who I have had the privilege to meet and work with at the Institute of Mindfulness and Transpersonal psychology, the Flame centre of Mindfulness, the retreats, workshops and courses, this work would never have been written.

This book is dedicated to those who have practically demonstrated, regaining control over their health and wellbeing, actualizing their human potential and inspiring others by practically applying the teachings in this book.

Introduction

In a world dominated, over loaded and over flowing with information, there has never been a need for humanity to rediscover the meaning and purpose in being human. It is the wisdom traditions that are now providing answers to our modern post truth life styles.

India is rich and diverse with its wisdom traditions, knowledge and practices relating to every aspect of health, covering the entire spectrum from physical, mental, emotional and spiritual health or authentic being. The foci of these incredible and invaluable knowledge-systems have been panhuman. They are applicable across humanity in the pursuit of liberating human beings from bondages of ego-centric, self-serving lives without meaning, purpose and subject to self inflicted suffering. Health and wellbeing are of primary importance to all human beings, its value being pan human. Health comprises of the physical, mental, emotional and spiritual dimensions of the human experience. Unhealthiness or dis-ease is experienced as suffering, a state of discomfort experienced at physically, mentally, emotionally and at the core of our being, as a sense of dis satisfaction, unsatisfactoriness. The Indian Wisdom traditions offer a variety of paths in cultivating optimum health, wellbeing. In particular, the Indian psychological models offer enormous implications for health, psychology, education, organizational management and human andsocial development.

What do we mean by Indian Psychology? Indian

psychology is an approach to psychology that is based on ideas and practices that developed over thousands of years within the Indian subcontinent.

Based on underlying philosophy, conceptual frameworks, methods of enquiry, and practices to access consciousness and to bring about psychological change and transformation in a safe and secure manner.[1]

Indian psychology is rooted in Indian ethos and thought, including the variety of psychological practices that exist in the country. Indian psychology is the study of embodied consciousness, or Jiva, it includes the holistic study and understanding of human nature, exploration and actualization of its latent potential for the optimum health and quality of life for the individual and society at large. In these models of health, wholeness, integration, connectivity, freedom, creativity and enjoyment are central to human existence. Cultivating optimum health comprises of a process consisting of three stages, first, regaining health, second, maintaining health and third, engaging in activities to cultivate optiumum health and wellbeing. Regaining health is effectively taking control of one's health, reducing and eliminating conditions which give rise to in incongruiety and malfunction. The second focuses on engaging in activities to maintain health and wellbeing, e.g Tai Chi, Aryveda, Yoga, Chi Kung and meditation. The third aspect focuses on activities that enhance cultivation of wellbeing, peace, harmony and freedom.[2]

Over the past 100 years because of British colonisation of India, the Indigenous knowledge-culture, that have been applied, studied and verified continuously was replaced and dominated by Freudian and behavioural approaches. During the time of the British rule in India, the British East India Company adopted a policy of funding only European-style education within its territories, with an aim to producing inidviduals who were brown on the outside, but English in their thinking.[4]

The imperial goal of Lord Macaulays for establishing "the impressible empire of our (European) arts and morals, literature and laws" resulted in dominating Indian knowledge systems and sadly continues in many Indian universities today. The tradition of spiritual self-development which gave psychology in India its most distinctive character enabling self actualisation, self realisation and finally self sovereignty was a threat to the British colonisers. (Minute by the Hon'ble T. B. Macaulay, dated the 2nd February 1835). The British administrators used Freudian psychology and behaviourism to "deal" with anyone who'd questioned the authority of their rule.[3,5]

Post 1947 following the independency of India, psychology continued to develop along behaviourist ideology, which now is beginning to show its limitations and its inability to actual deal with the real issues of human suffering and are exposing themselves as externally controlling psychological approaches.[3]

What makes Indian psychology distinct and separate from Western approaches is that they stand as a body of knowledge grounded and pursued with different ontological and epistemological premises, taking a fundamental spiritual growth perspective on human development and growth.

Over the past decade or so, the paradigm has started to change, attitudes and perceptions of Indian psychology is growing exponentially amongst not only psychologists in India, but now across the western world as Mindfulness, compassion based approaches that are demonstrating themselves to be highly effective against stress, chronic pain, depression, anxiety and a whole variety of mental health issues.

The tried and tested models from Indian psychology, offer a gold mine for building a more comprehensive and applicable approach human health well being and evolution. Gurmat is the latest knowledge-system from the rich mines of Indian civilisation which has brought the world a whole range of time tested systems such as yoga, Ayurveda, Buddhist psychology, etc.

In contrast to the Western framework, Gurmat provides a framework applicable across cultures. The assumption base of Gurmat psychology includes:

The Charpadarath or the four essential life pursuits that every human being endeavours to fulfil in life, Artha, Kama, Dharma and Moksha.

Artha is material prosperity, kama is emotional fulfilment, dharma is ethical conduct and responsibilities, and Moksha is liberation from ego-bound bondage and attachments. Attachments are the source of human suffering, attachments give rise to desires, desires give rise to hope, fear and anger, fear and anger gives rise to mindlessness, mindlessness blinds one from the preciousness of one's finite life. The Char-Padarath covers the entire range of human possibilities and provides practical guidance and communal infrastructure to enable the personal self-actualisation and self-realisation within the Sikh way of life.

Gurmat conceives the human being as a unique composite of body, mind and consciousness. Unlike Western psychology in which consciousness is considered as epiphenomena[7], Gurmat considers Consciousness central to human being. It is changeless and permanent base of all awareness and knowledge. Consciousness enables human beings' personal freedom and subjectivity, enabling every human being with an opportunity to exercise their personal intention and to experience joy and blissfulness in life.

The mind like the body is material although subtle unlike the gross physical body. It is the interface between consciousness and the body. Because of mis-understanding or ignorance, the ever-changing temporal world that is given greater significance and value, than ones' embodied consciousness or Jiv Atma. This ignorance binds ones' conditioned sense of self, Haumai (see later), with the ever-changing material world through attachments (Moh) that create the conditions necessary for human suffering. Through Gyan or knowledge from an individual who is themselves self-realised, conscious and self-sovereign or Sat Guru one dispels the fog of ignorance to enter unknown stages and states of consciousness beyond the conditioned sense of self towards the Sacred self.

Gurmat presents existence, including every human being as a manifestation of Divinity as well as the essential self in every being. This sense of sacred equality is again panhuman and universal, which influences, motivates and inspires one to be of service to others (sewa) within the sacred Existence. Gurmat gyan combined with practises empower individuals to address their root cause of suffering.

In contrast to Western mind and body dualism, Gurmat, is founded on mind body monoism or direct connection between mind and body, with consciousness as its centrality as opposed to ego and cultivation of daily practises of meditation and selflessness actions.

The centrality of consciousness and daily practices (rehat) are foundational within Gurmat and provide the understanding of human transformation, the causes and the consequences (karma) of mindless and mindfulness actions and provide the methods and means of transforming the individual in pursuit of authenticity, as being (sat), centrality in knowing or awareness (chit or gur) and Joyfulness, (experienced as non-dual, non-verbal, pure consciousness), (Anand or parshad).

Gurmat emphasises the cultivation of positive psychology or Gunn through personal training and practises (rehat) that enable a human being to overcome and transform the unhealthy psychological states such as depression, anxiety, stress, fear and anger into healthier and wholesome states such as contentment, self-compassion, compassion, gratitude, hope, optimism founded on personal ethics.

Ethical responsibility through action and consequences or karma is another element that is panhuman and universal. Karma in its two simplest form, accumulate conditioning (sanchit) and those actions currently underway, conditioned behaviour (prarabdha) demonstrate human behaviour as an evolving process through time, tying the conditioned sense of self or haumai as the engine behind karma. Gurmat takes this into account, thus the mind, its intention, actions, place and time (lehka) in considering personal ethics.

Gurmat teachings make an important contribution to the science of mental health and provide a perennial form of healing which includes the realisation of the eternal, limitless sacred nature of the Self beyond the confines of the ego-complex (haumai).

Gurmat is the latest comprehensive psycho-spiritual health and well-being systems to emerge from the East, adding to the excellent health systems found within Buddhist psychology (Abidharam), Yoga or Aryveda.

Gurmat is a highly-sophisticated time tested psycho-spiritual approach to psychological, physical and spiritual health and well-being. Its methods and practises have been used over centuries to test, experiment and experientially validate the higher states of consciousness. Its comprehensive approach enables the cultivation of healthy self-development and transformation enabling self-actualisations, self-realisation and finally self-sovereignty for the practitioners.

Gurmat provides a consciousness based approach, with contemplative practises which help individuals recognise the workings of their mind, its impact of their physiology and processes for recognising, transforming and transcending it. Gurmat provides a safe and secure process for both personal and transpersonal development.

This book introduces Gurmat as a psycho-spiritual approach to developing healthy individuals who can make a constructive life affirming contribution to society.

This book is because of all those who have been helped through this approach to not only regain their health, but also to develop into strong, confident and productive purposeful human beings.

CHAPTER ONE

World View, Identity and Key Concepts

Gurmat – Psycho-spiritual therapy for personal and transpersonal transformation

If there was ever a time in Human history to seek an alternative to the ego dominated, insatiable greed led behaviour in the world, it is today! Today, being human, particularly within predatory capitalist societies is nothing more than a debt burdened slave, who sacrifice their lives, health, relationships in the pursuit of "happiness" and collection of material objects, which, while one may have spent a lifetime accumulating, are likely to end up in nothing more than jumble sale upon one's death.

So, what is the point of our life? To collect "stuff" or to continuous strive for the illusion of "happiness" yet not quiet ever getting there, or waiting for things to get better or simply slaving away until you die?

Unfortunately, there is no formal or adequate education system in the developed world which addresses the central questions about what it is to be human and the development of human potential. Almost all education offered at schools, colleges and universities is geared towards conditioning individuals into what to think, rather than how to think or to actualise and fulfil human potential.

Today, we find as the predatory debt ridden systems begin to collapse around us, society is discovering that it has been misled and betrayed. It's been betrayed by its religions and their leaders, betrayed by the illusion of financial security, betrayed by the "elected" Governments, bankers, food manufacturers and the pharmaceutical industries, all of whom have placed profit above life and the environment. This out-dated ego centric model of measuring human life in terms of material wealth has brought destruction and pollution to every life system on earth.

This corrupt predominantly materialist, Abrahamic and ego-centric worldview has misled and misdirected humanity away from the dignity of being human, conditioned behaviour towards sensory gratification and accumulating material as "wealth". Within this paradigm, Human life has been financialised; it is measured in terms of money, power, status and prestige without any appreciation or acknowledgement of the greater human potential. The Judeo-Christian and Abrahamic worldviews in which Existence is distinct, value free, objective, machine line, material, separate from "God" and grounded in dualism has significantly contributed to the predatory capitalism and the exploitation of all life, environment and human beings. The assumption of the superiority and privilege of the Christian "white man" over all other races and life was imposed through the colonisation of other cultures and foreably enforced.[4]

While most of us are engaged in an endless effort towards creating a sense of happiness, or lasting satisfaction and while we all chase and seek this "happiness", yet most of us have a distorted and deluded idea of what might bring happiness, let alone know it. In our ignorance, we don't recognise that the sense of happiness tends to be momentary and temporary thus insatiable and impermanent. Considering this, it may be a more accurate definition to recognise its not happiness that is being chased, but a constant attempt to make things different to experience a sense of s̟ pleasantness, fulfilment and purpose.

Motivated with an insatiable desire to achieve "happiness" or "greater happiness" in fulfilling our priorities we are unaware how entrenched we become in accumulating objects, chasing fame, prestige and wealth. In return, we sacrifice our health, relationships and wellbeing for a life experience dominated by stress, anxiety, depression, and ill health. So, One may ask, what is the point? The answer is understanding what you really need, recognising the desires that are motivating you and learning to express your human potential for what it is! Unfortunately, most have little or no understanding of what it means to be human, let alone what to do to fulfil its complete potential.

In an age dominated by technology, communication and information most are ignorant of the constant conditioning underway, creating emotional and cognitive dissonance in the minds of the Screen-glued-senses that keep the senses distracted To make matters worse, the current mindset is so heavily influenced, conditioned and manipulated that it's a miracle that one is able to see through these veils of dis-information about being human, and a far cry from what is happiness or what is likely to bring lasting happiness.

To truly express and fulfil your human potential, we need to begin by understanding ourselves and in doing so, recognise the role of our senses, our conditioned mind and the mental lens through which we "see" the world and ourselves. When we begin to peel away various layers to reveal what we truly are, our innate nature, our "mool roop", essential nature and , we discover the nature of our mind, its conditioned states, how it creates ones' inner realities and as we progress in this life changing and life enhancing journey, we discover the illusion of happiness, the illusion of suffering and ultimately, arriving our essential sense of self, beyond your sense of ego-complex, expressed as Self-aware, continuous, interconnected joyful life or Anand.

Have you ever considered why you are alive? What did you do to deserve your life, to be born in a family, to a certain mother and father, in a set location, race, gender, colour and physique? What does it mean to be human? What is your human potential? How do you achieve your potential, happiness, contentment, a sense of peace and purpose in your life?

> Gourree Mehalaa 1 ||
> Jaatho Jaae Kehaa Thae Aavai ||
> Keh Oupajai Keh Jaae Samaavai ||
> Kio Baadhhiou Kio Mukathee Paavai ||
> Kio Abinaasee Sehaj Samaavai ||1||
> How can we know where we came from?
> From where we originate, and where will we merge?
> How are we bound, and how do we liberate?
> How do we merge with intuitive ease into the Eternal,
>   Imperishable Oneness? ||1||

(Raag Gauri Guru Nanak Dev Ang:152)

These are the central questions addressed in the Sikh philosophy and practical teachings contained in the Sri Guru Granth Sahib, the primary authoritative sacred text of the Sikh Gurus, Bhagats and Mystics, the Bodhisattvas of Punjab. The Sri Guru Granth Sahib is an ocean of profound knowledge, wisdom and contains within it both the nature of reality, as well as the nature of being human. What is being presented in this book is a glimpse into a psycho-spiritual approach to human development, growth and conscious evolution. The teaching from sacred Sikh texts focus on the mind and life style from a psycho-spiritual stand point. Engagement with life is based on an ethical stand point, which becomes a foundational hall mark of human health, well being and function per Gurmat.

This publication is an attempt to present an outline of a psycho-spiritual therapeutic approach to cultivating optimum health and well-being, Sahej. Gurmat (Gur=awareness, teacher; Mat= understanding, wisdom, psychology) is based on Sikh teachings, it is the Sikh equivalent of Abidharam or Buddhist psychology. Gurmat presents a highly progressive, practical, transformative and life-engaging worldview; it contains a psycho-spiritual model which at its core has a sacred dimension. It presents a psycho-spiritual process of self-development and transpersonal growth in an interconnected sacred Universe in which model of human being is a multi-layered and tri-dimensional psycho-physical-spiritual, an energetic sacred phenomenon of life, an embedded consciousness in the eternal ever present Nowness.

While both Gurmat and Buddhism see the conditioned mind, (hau) ego-complex as an illusionary sense of self and the cause of bondage to both suffering and the cycle of birth and death. Gurmat goes beyond the excellent psychological teachings contained in the Buddhist traditions to provide a psycho-spiritual dimension not as a second, separate "God" but within the context of One, non-dual interconnected joyful consciousness unfolding into myriads of forms. Gurmat asserts a human being without ego (hau) or sense of separate self, is no different to "God", the drop recognizes its waterness within the ocean".

ਇਹੁ ਮਨੁ ਨਿਰਮਲੁ ਹਉਮੈ ਮਾਰੀ ॥

Ih mann nirmal haumai maaree.

Gurmat asserts that Jeeva (individual being) without ego (Haumai) becomes Godlike.

(SGGS 1049)

ਜਬ ਹਮ ਹੋਤੇ ਤਬ ਤੂ ਨਾਹੀ ਅਬ ਤੁਹੀ ਮੈ ਨਾਹੀ ॥
ਅਨਲ ਅਗਾਮ ਜੈਸੇ ਲਹਰਿ ਮਇ ਓਦਧਿ ਜਲ ਕੇਵਲ ਜਲ ਮਾਂਹੀ ॥੧॥

Jab Ham Hothae Thab Thoo Naahee Ab Thoohee Mai
Naahee ॥
Anal Agam Jaisae Lehar Mae Oudhadhh Jal Kaeval Jal
Maanhee ॥1॥

When ego is present, then You are not, Now You are
present, ego is not
The wind may raise up huge waves in the vast ocean, but
they are just water in water. ॥1॥

(Raag Sorath Bhagat Ravidas 657)

Gurmat offers us a comprehensive understanding of
the nature of reality, insights into the psycho-spiritual nature
of being human, and practical processes designed to
cultivate optimum holistic health and fulfilment of human
potential towards self-actualisation and self-realisation.

Gurmat focuses on the transformation of ego-bound
identities into self-sovereign, self-realised integral holistic
sacred beings.

ਬਲਿਹਾਰੀ ਗੁਰ ਆਪਣੇ ਦਿਉਹਾੜੀ ਸਦ ਵਾਰ ॥
ਜਿਨਿ ਮਾਣਸ ਤੇ ਦੇਵਤੇ ਕੀਏ ਕਰਤ ਨ ਲਾਗੀ ਵਾਰ ॥੧॥

Balihaaree Gur Aapanae Dhiouhaarree Sadh Vaar ॥
Jin Maanas Thae Dhaevathae Keeeae Karath N Laagee
Vaar ॥1॥

A hundred times a day, I am a sacrifice to my Guru;
He made angels out of men, without delay. ॥1॥

(Raag Asa Guru Nanak Dev Ang:462)

Sri Guru Grant Sahib, was compiled in 1604, contained
in 1430 pages of unadultered sacred teachings of individuals
who have themselves undergone ego-development, ego-
transformation, ego-transcendence and experience non-
dual state as pure consciousness. It provides a unique
insight into the fullness of what it means to be "human". A
quick check of the 1430 pages provides you with a glimpse

of its content with regard human development, consciousness and suffering.

	'Man' Mind	'Hau- mai' 'Ahankar' Ego	'Purekh' 'Jot' Conscious- ness	'Dukh' Suffer- ing	'Dhyan' 'Symran' Medi- tation	Anand Non-dual conscious- ness
No. of references in SGGS	4985	1126	970	725	2840	348

Gurmat, the teachings of the Gurus, bring together, experiential worldview, time tested wisdom on the nature of existence, human mind, and practical techniques. This combination provides a highly sophisticated and yet a practical approach to eliminating physical, psychological and existential suffering; Provide an opportunity to transcend the self-limiting mental sense of "I"-amness. Through practical approaches that enable the cultivation of optimum health and the fulfillment of our human potential.

The initial practice begins with calming the mind, and experience a sense of peace, tranquillity or contentment through symran or correct-mindfulness.

Just as a flame can only be lit by an existing flame, the same is true for authentic masters.

Correct mindfulness is the practise of mindfulness as taught by a teacher with lineage and with an accurate understanding of the nature of Reality, mind and Existence, including actual experience of non-dual unified pure consciousness experience.

Contentment provides the first rung on the ladder of gradual ego-recognition, ego-transformation and ego-transcendence ultimately towards self-realisation enabling individuals to awakening to themselves, their relationship to others, nature and unveiling their own sacredness.

Gurmat focuses on the self-transformation of ordinary ego focused human experience into non-dual consciousness experience by transcending the ego-complex through simple yet practical contemplative practices and experientially examining the nature of reality and life.

These practical teachings make an important contribution to the science of mental health and provide a perennial form of healing which includes the realisation of the eternal, limitless sacred nature of the Self beyond the confines of the ego-complex.

Those who are fortunate enough to be exposed to Gurmat teachings and practices will discover, realise and experience physical, psychological and spiritual health and wellbeing through:

Recognising and understanding the nature of Reality

Recognising and understanding the nature of our mind, our ego-complex in creating our subjective experiences

Recognising, understanding the nature of suffering(Dukh), its causes and solutions.

Recognising, understanding and cultivating healthy psychological states

Recognising, understanding and transforming unhealthy psychological states

Recognising the physiological damage of sustained unhealthy psychological states

Practical experiential contemplative exercises for the cultivation of present moment awareness, contentment, compassion, internal ethics and values, generosity, peaceand authenticity

Practical experiential contemplative exercises totranscend ego-complex and unveil sacredness throughPresence

Recognising and cultivating fullness of human potential and purpose

Gurmat provides a staged process which begins with the cultivation of a healthy ego-complex by recognizing reducing and transforming conditioned and unhealthy psychological states through correct-mindfulness based contemplative practices. This leads to greater mental clarity and the recognition of the ego-complex (Hau) and its role in everyday life, which is essential to ego-transformation, transcendence and transpersonal development.

ਹਉਮੈ ਬੁਝੈ ਤਾ ਦਰੁ ਸੁਝੈ ॥

Houmai Boojhai Thaa Dhar Soojhai ||

When the ego-body complex is known, then the doorway is recognised.

(Raag Asa Guru Nanak Dev Ang:466 Line: 15)

Gurmat addresses the development of healthy psychological states which begin with the cultivation of contentment through present moment awareness, giving rise to compassion. Contentment and compassion can be considered as the parents of Dharma, personal ethical and responsible lifestyle.

This process of self-transformation and development ultimately leads to a continued sense of gratitude, a unified sense of self and its selflessness expression in everyday life.

Gurmat offers a safe and practical approach towards the next stage of human development, that of ego-transcendence and the transpersonal transformational process.

Gurmat recognise the monism of mind and body, in contrast to the dualism in Western psychology and world view.

Gurmat holds Consciousness (Akal Purekh) and individualised consciousness (jiv atma) central as opposed to ego (haumai)

Gurmat focus on daily practises of meditation and self-awareness known as Rehat, as part of life style rather than a quick fix to a goal!

Unlike the Western scientific worldview, which considers life and existence to be a mere accident, Gurmat considers Existence as sacred and life as a most precious time bound gift, which provides a rare opportunity for individualised consciousness to know itself.

Unfortunately, because of ignorance on the part of individuals and the deliberate manipulation and conditioning right from birth, combined with unavailability and access to a teacher of life, a Guru, both life and health are sacrificed in pursuit of worthless agendas, accumulation of material wealth and chasing some distant idea of happiness.

This human life is the most precious of gifts, yet through ignorance of self, attachment to ones' ego-complex is wasted in pursuit of objects of desire and temporary gratification.

> gourree bairaagan mehalaa 1 ||
> rain gavaaee soe kai dhivas gavaaeiaa khaae ||
> heerae jaisaa janam hai kouddee badhalae jaae ||1||

> Gauree Bairaagan, First Mehla:
> The nights are wasted sleeping, and the days are wasted eating.
> Human life is such a precious jewel, but it is being lost in exchange for a mere shell. ||1||

> (Guru Nanak Dev 156)

Before we move towards unpacking Gurmat as a psycho-spiritual therapy, it is important to know the context within which the psych-spiritual model has been developed. Gurmat developed in the north-west region of India called Punjab. India is extremely rich in its sciences, philosophies andtraditions such as Buddhism, Vendanta, Sankaya, Vaisheshika, Nyaya, Mimasa and Yoga. Each school of philosophy contains its own inherent psychological models and systems developed over several thousand years of human experience. It is essential to recognise the crucial differences between Eastern psychology and Western psychology and their approach to human function, development and potential.

The book has been structured into two sections, the first deals with Gurmat, its worldview and nature of teachings contrasted with Western worldview. The second section will be devoted to Gurmat psycho-spiritual model and approach towards optimum health and transpersonal growth.

Gurmat transforms at least three distinct elements in human development, namely psychology, physiology including neurology and cultivation of authenticity and consciousness (spirituality as beyond the ego-self). Through contemplative attention and awareness development practices, together with recognition and understanding the essential nature of reality, Gurmat provides every human being with opportunity to develop their full human potential and function, as a lived experience rather than a mental belief system.

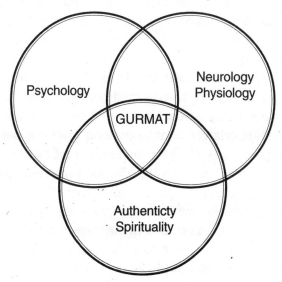

Difference between Eastern and Western worldview and psychology

Let us begin with worldviews, the fundamental view of reality within Western psychology and contrast this with Eastern view of reality. Our worldview is our perception of "reality", our mind-set which includes our self and our self-image. In other words, it is how we see the world and our existence within it. Worldview is not something that we are born with, but it is gradually constructed and developed within us as our mental model of reality through interaction with "external" stimulus, schooling and social engagement.

These interactions begin with basic needs for food, warmth and safety. However, as our engagement and interaction develop and increase with parents,language, schooling, religion and society, we begin to create our mental model of reality, the lens through which we "see" the world, our worldview.

Our worldview is created, maintained and reinforced through a whole range of channels and it is of specific interest to those wishing to exploit others. The channels used to create, maintain and reinforce worldviews include language and re-definition of words and concepts, mind-conditioning systems such as schools, colleges, universities, and religions all of which use methods to create the mental model of our reality by teaching us to think in a particular way and more importantly what to exclude from our paradigm.

Religions, especially the dualist Judeo-Christian models of religion, further enforce the division between individuals and the authoritarian figure of a distant "God". Those in position of authority within the religious institution then can exploit the automated self-preservation conditioning of individuals, manipulating their behaviour and action to seek pleasures in heaven and avoid the pain of hell, as seen in the growth of violent religious radicalisation. This distorted worldview is reinforced and maintained through the constant exposure to selected information of emotive and fear driven "news" designed to maintain individuals in ignorance.[9,10,11,12] Gurmat refers to the mental conditioning as "maal", filth, stain, or pollution which helps create our separated sense of self, Hau (ego-complex) and our sense of the world, dividing "me" from the "other" into a dualistic worldview. Thus, our subjective point of view, creates duality. (Discussed further below)

ਮਨ ਕਰਹਲਾ ਅਤਿ ਨਿਰਮਲਾ ਮਲੁ ਲਾਗੀ ਹਉਮੈ ਆਇ ॥

Man Karehalaa Ath Niramalaa Mal Laagee Houmai Aae ||

O camel-like mind, you were once very pure; the filth of egotism has now attached itself to you.

(Raag Gauri Poorbee Guru Ram Das)

Our worldview is of critical importance, as it determines our engagement as well as our outcome in life.It is vital and of primary importance in the field of psychology for these very reasons, engagement and outcome. The Gurmat worldview is significantly different from the materialistic, mechanical and dualistic western model of the universe and life as accidents; Gurmat encompasses the growth and development of human potential beyond ego development and ego-fixation. Gurmat provides a comprehensive and tested approach to human development through far reaching understanding of Existence, human potential and practical processes including correct-mindfulness, transcendental meditation practices and activities designed to help transcend ego-centric based activities.

At a psychological level, these experiential practices and teachings transform our worldview, enable the cultivation of positive emotions of contentment, mental tranquillity, compassion, self-compassion, gratitude, refined intellect, expressed through ethical and self-aware behaviour.

The worldview of western psychology is exclusively materialist and atomistic, which sees reality as an inert mechanical universe, predictable, blind, purposeless, life as an accident and where psychology is the automatic response to external stimuli, and human beings are separate physical entities living in a physical mechanical universe as reality. The Western scientific mindset of the past 200 hundred years has increasingly dominated the worldview of our modern society and in particular the dominance of western psychological models as a "fits-all" for every culture in the world. This not only demonstrates the arrogance behind this materialistic worldview, but also a culture that should have vanished with the disappearance of colonialism.[13]

Colonisation operated by dividing colonized populations "into manageable parts,". The British used psychology to accomplish this in a different way than the familiar classifications of race, caste, and tribe. Divide and rule played a central role in British rule, whether by revealing variation within groups through mental testing or universal forces of desire and conflict through psychoanalysis.[4]

The rich Eastern wisdom traditions concerned with consciousness and self-development were labelled as primitive and backwards, and replaced with the supposed superior western methods, concepts and objective knowledge.

Great improvements have been made in the areas of technology, urban development and medicine. However, the consequences of the arrogant colonial attitude as a dominated worldview, have had a devastating and detrimental impact on human health, life systems and the environment. Without exception, the predatory and exploitative economic system of the Western world has now impacted multiple aspects of life on the planet, polluting water, air, food, ground and the oceans.

The Western worldview and its insatiable economic model is no different from a parasitic disease or cancer, it's based on exploitation for the sake of "profit", which is measured by numbers on bank balances, clothes, cars, material wealth and the status they hold. This lack of understanding and thus inconsideration towards self, others and the environment divides one from not only others, but also creates a division within ourselves, which we are constantly and actively discouraged from exploring.

This harmful worldview is both contradictory and illusionary, for example, on the one hand promoting human rights, while on the other exploiting those very humans, creating ever new types of weaponry, destructive machinery against life on the land, air or water. A blatant disregard for life, ignorant of being human but continuing to inflict untold suffering across the planet. This greed-fuelled ego gratification has only strengthened and reinforced ego-fixation at our individual, national, racial and religious levels, in addition to creating cognitive dissonance within us through conflicting attitudes, beliefs and behaviour against intuitive knowing.

Gurmat recognise the ego-fixation or deluded-mind as the chronic disease of modern man which is not only wasting a most precious gift of life but destroying the planet, poisoning the oceans and polluting the air in pursuit of "happiness", mindless addiction to accumulate objects which will inevitable prove to be worthless in the certainty of death.

Gurmat recognises the profound damage of an ego-dominated life and offers both understanding and practical methods to help regain balance of oneself first, through the cultivation of a healthier ego-complex and the healthy interaction and engagement with the others and the environment. This is not taught behaviour, but cultivated from within oneself through the appropriate practises and teachings.

In ignorance, our ego-complex (Hau) fuelled by craving or "trisanaa" (object oriented craving) for its own satisfaction, creates a self-reinforcing psychological pattern, chasing one object of desire to another in pursuit of happiness, comfort or gratification. This thirst for own egoic satisfaction creates attachment to transitory pleasures. The indulgence in gratification of these egoic pleasures produces both the growth and continuation of self-hood or "I"-am-ness.

ਅਹੰਕਾਰੁ ਤਿਸਨਾ ਰੋਗੁ ਲਗਾ ਬਿਰਥਾ ਜਨਮੁ ਗਵਾਵਹੇ ॥

Ahankaar Thisanaa Rog Lagaa Birathhaa Janam Gavaavehae ॥

You are afflicted with the diseases of ego and craving, and you are wasting your life away in vain.

(Ang 441 Line 8 Raag Asa: Guru Amar Das)

In the West, the authority of religion has been replaced with science. Religion as a belief system has been replaced by scientism, where anything reported by "scientific authority" is accepted and believed as truth without question, creating an acceptance where authority becomes the truth, rather than truth being the authority.

The disregard for consciousness within western psychology has completely distorted western psychology, replacing processes and practices for human development, actualisation, ego-transcendence and self-realisation with simply "ego-fixing". The field of western psychology is focused on changing behaviour through conditioning a "healthier" ego or mental model of your reality but not addressing the very fact that you have a mind, but are not the mind! This has created several errors inherent in western psychology including mind-body separation which has blinded the link between psychological states, physiology and disease, ignorant of the therapeutic power of awareness in relationship to mental illness and trauma.

Over the past two decades, western psychology has been undergoing a silent revolution, such that the comtemplative practices considered "primitive" and "irrelevant" to health and wellbeing have indeed stood the test of time and demonstrated to have profound therapeutic efficacy within main stream psychology.

Meditation, particularly, mindfulness use has grown exponentially within the therapeutic settings, such that mindfulness based interventions have provided effective solutions for pain management, depression, ADHD, anxiety, stress management and even recovery from head and brain injuries.

Other comtemplative practices such as yoga, Chi kung, tai chi, and compassion based interventions are getting established within main stream therapy. This can be seen through the out standing growth in meditation based smart phone apps.

Additionally, it is becoming increasingly obvious the value of spirituality and religion in health and wellbeing. Abundant evidence is available on the robust relationship between spirituality and religion with health and wellbeing.

Peer-Reviewed Research

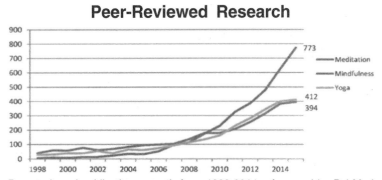

Peer reviewed publications growth from 1998-2014 referenced by PubMed

Gurmat psychology clearly distinguishes healthy from unhealthy psychological states, provides awareness based practices to initiate, heal psychological trauma, and develop internal resilience that can be developed through a staged inner journey of transpersonal growth beyond ego-identification. Ultimately, the goal of human life per Gurmat psychology is to know oneself, and recognise ones'sacred innate nature.

ਇਉ ਕਹੈ ਨਾਨਕੁ ਮਨ ਤੂੰ ਜੋਤਿ ਸਰੂਪੁ ਹੈ ਅਪਨਾ ਮੂਲੁ ਪਛਾਣੁ ॥੫॥

Iou kahai Nanaku man toon joti saroopu hai apanaa moolu pashaanu ll5ll

Thus says Nanak - O mind! Your "Saroop" (your own, True State) is "Joti" (Divine Light)! Recognize your original nature (Source, Origin, Reality...) ll5ll

(SGGS 441)

Gurmat worldview declares there is but One AbsoluteReality (param-atma, Naam, Akal Purekh, Braham), pureconsciousness, infinite and homogeneous oneness whichis the substratum ("Adhaar") of all existence, in Nowness This is the foundational and primary reality, and is the conscious Self, the Jeev Atma, or embodied consciousness in all living beings.

ਤੂੰ ਦਰੀਆਉ ਸਭ ਤੁਝ ਹੀ ਮਾਹਿ ॥
ਤੁਝ ਬਿਨੁ ਦੂਜਾ ਕੋਈ ਨਾਹਿ ॥
ਜੀਅ ਜੰਤ ਸਭਿ ਤੇਰਾ ਖੇਲੁ ॥

Thoon Dhareeaao Sabh Thujh Hee Maahi ll
Thujh Bin Dhoojaa Koee Naahi ll
Jeea Janth Sabh Thaeraa Khael ll

You are the River of Life; all are within You.
There is no one except You.
All living beings are Your playthings.

(Raag Asa Guru Ram Das Ang:11)

All beings are in this Self, and the Self is in all beings. All forms emerge out of this Conscious Principle, sustained by this Conscious Principle, and ultimately merge back into this Conscious Principle. Existence is a spontaneous-continuous-cyclic-unfolding process, expressed as birth, growth, death, re-birth ad-infinitum following natural-intrinsic-order.

ਸਲੋਕੁ ॥
ਨਿਰੰਕਾਰ ਆਕਾਰ ਆਪਿ ਨਿਰਗੁਨ ਸਰਗੁਨ ਏਕ ॥
ਏਕਹਿ ਏਕ ਬਖਾਨਨੋ ਨਾਨਕ ਏਕ ਅਨੇਕ ॥੧॥

Shalok:

Nirankaar Aakaar Aap Niragun Saragun Eaek ||~

Eaekehi Eaek Bakhaanano Naanak Eaek Anaek ||1||

Formless and form One without attributes and with attributes

Describe the Oneness as One, and Only One; O Nanak, One, yet infinite forms. ||1||

(Raag Gauri Guru Arjan Dev Ang: 250)

ਪੰਚ ਤਤੁ ਸੁੰਨਹੁ ਪਰਗਾਸਾ ॥
ਦੇਹ ਸੰਜੋਗੀ ਕਰਮ ਅਭਿਆਸਾ ॥

Panch Thath Sunnahu Paragaasaa ||

Dhaeh Sanjogee Karam Abhiaasaa ||

From Primal Void (Silence) the five elements manifested. They joined to form the body, which engages in actions.

(Raag Maaroo Guru Nanak Dev Ang:)

Per Gurmat, the physical manifested universe is fundamentally composed of five elements, earth (solid), water (liquid), air (gas-fluid), fire (plasma, radiation) and space/ether (dark matter), the relatively "empty-ness", interconnected-quantum-field. The mind is not separate from the body or different from matter, it is matter albeit a subtle form of matter

ਪੰਚ ਤਤੁ ਕਰਿ ਤੁਧੁ ਸ੍ਰਿਸਟਿ ਸਭ ਸਾਜੀ
ਕੋਈ ਛੇਵਾ ਕਰਿਉ ਜੇ ਕਿਛੁ ਕੀਤਾ ਹੋਵੈ ॥

Panch Thath Kar Thudhh Srisatt Sabh Saajee

Koee Shhaevaa Kario Jae Kishh Keethaa Hovai ||

You created the entire Universe out of the five elements;
if anyone can create a sixth, let him.

(Raag Suhi Guru Ram Das Ang:736)

ਇਹੁ ਮਨੁ ਪੰਚ ਤਤੁ ਤੇ ਜਨਮਾ ॥

Eihu Man Panch Thath Thae Janamaa ॥

This mind is born of the five elements.

(Raag Asa Guru Nanak Dev Ang: 415 Line: 10)

Our worldview (drisiti) is the single most important influence on the way we interpret our experiences and respond to those experiences. The table below provides the contrast between

Eastern – Wisdom - Tradition Worldview	Western – Modern Cartesian Worldview
More than 3000 years of subjective expereince– holistic concept of mind and health expressed as self-actualising lifestyle	Less than 150 years of "scientific psychology" systematic scientific study of experience and behaviour
Certrality of Consciousness-unified as absolute Existence, consciousness and joy – Sat Chit Anand	Exclusive materialistic world view, dualistic Consciouness an epiphenomena of brain
Non-dual interconnected energetic vibrating multi-verse, manifesting as myriads of form	Reductionist framework with sharp distinction between mind and body, material and spiritual – other dualisms
Integrated approach to knowledge Intensely practical Understanding, knowing, Being	Explaining, predicting and controlling behaviour analysing, gathering knowledge

Eastern – Wisdom - Tradition Worldview	Western – Modern Cartesian Worldview
Concerned with nature of essential being, part of Existence in harmony with environment and others, recognising and transcending ego	Concerned with personality growth of individual developing ego, individualisation and power
Knowledge liberates	Knowledge is power
self-actualisation development of healthy integrated ego-development, followed by Ego-transcendence and unification	Individualisation of ego followed by ego-fixing
Sanction for selflessness	Sanction for selfishness
Subjective, in deterministic and ethical	Objective, deterministic and value free
Coherent knowledge system with over 3000 years of subjective experiential validation	Disparate knowledge system
Life – purposeful, evolutionary and pathway to self-sacredness	Life, blind, purposeless and an accident!
Psycho-spiritual continuum, expressed in duality of material and consciousness, yet intrinsically one	Anti-spiritual and materlistic

The table below highlights how "religious" worldviews, level of self-awareness and psychological states. The first four religious worldviews are primarily *Abrahamic* religions, while the latter three are consciousness based Indic traditions such as Buddhist, Sikh and Hindu worldviews.

Types of Religions	World View	Outcome	Ego-types Ego-fixation	Awareness
Ignorance-oriented	Belief systems to protect ego	Fanatic	Body self food and sex	Self-preservation Identity - Hau
Fear-oriented	Fear of "hell', and buried continuous repression: Continious avoidance, the don't do's	God as the punisher Afraid of life, afraid to live	Self-Identity I-am-ness Haumai	Body Suffering Aversion
Greed-oriented	Greed for heaven, continuously "doing" to enter heaven, earning points to enter heaven	God the gatekeeper Waiting to "live"	Self-esteem I-the doer saint and sinners	Self-Esteem Pleasure Attraction

Types of Religions	World View	Outcome	Ego-types Ego-fixation	Awareness
Logic-orientated	logic, calculation, cleverness, worldly, materialistic, opportunistic, intellectual, theoretical, scriptural, traditional.	Pundits, Religious scholars God as theology "I" am	Self-extension "me" and "mine" Ahamkara	Self-relating Knowledge
Intelligence-oriented	Synthesizers, union, connectivity	God as presence, love, union SAT	Self-Image	Self-discovery
Meditation-con-sciousness-oriented	To "be", to know oneself	Self-realization God as Con-sciousness CHIT-GUR	Self-knowledge	Self-expression
Samadhi-life-oriented	Joy, celebration, song, dance, ecstasy	God as life in joy and ecstasy ANAND-PARSHAD	Mystics	Being
Conditioned belief system religions, ego and consciousness				

Gurmat differs significantly from the outdated and incomplete materialistic worldview from Western psychology, that has resulted in the distorting the understanding of consciousness,mind, ego and life purpose. In fact, the current dominant western worldview is effectively designed to harvest and exploit life for personal gain, a financialized life. The table below highlighting the significant differences in worldview regarding consciousness and life goal between the two paradigms.

Gurmat Psychological Worldview	Western Psychological Worldview
Consciousness-unified as absolute Existence, consciousness and joy – Sat Chit Anand	Exclusive materialistic world view Atomistic View
Subjective and emotive nature of "Anand"	"Just a bunch of neurons"
Mind-body connection Mind subtle form of matter	Mind-body disconnected, mind is somehow separate from physical existence (dualism) Dualistic division of mind and body
Consciouness as onthological Four states of consciousness waking (jågrata) dreaming (svapna) and deep sleep (sufupti) Turiya (meaning "the fourth") experience of pure conscious-ness.	Consciousness an epiphenomena, a by-product of the brain, Predictable yet also the –"the hard problem"
Defined Mind with identified elements and function Thought Memory/intention Discrimination - intellect "Ahamkaar - I-am-creator"	Limited understanding of mind and its functions Mind, ego, self, awareness, consciousness – undefined and interchangeable

Gurmat Psychological Worldview	Western Psychological Worldview
Freedom of response	Psychology – automatic response to external stimuli
Practical methods to enhance quality and reliability of inner observation Knowing the mind as the mind transcending ego-complex	Changing content of thoughts rather than seeing thoughts, emotions and sensations as transitory events Western psychology unable to move beyond ego-complex, psychotherapy limited to ego-fixing
Goal – integrated ethical way to bring entire life more in harmony with the highest we can conceive and experientially realise Recognising ego-complex, transcending Ego-complex into Pure Consciousness Experience and expressing unified integrated (selfless-ness) lifestyle	Goal – developing, defining personality, individualisation, self-assertion and domination

Gurmat, is a therapy in the sense that it has a practical approach and theory as how suffering comes about and it has a range of practises (as a lifestyle) designed to alleviate this condition, and it is specifically psychotherapeutic in that it sees the mind as playing a crucial role in this process.

While we are all busy gathering knowledge about everything from galaxies right through to the quantum nature of matter, yet hardly anyone can truly answer the question as to "what they really are". Our conditioned sense of self although functional, is a far truth from knowing what our intrinsic or essential nature (atam gyan) is. Through a systematic approach, Gurmat therapy helps uncover the various layers of our make-up such that one can experience the unbound interconnected and authentic sense of self, awareness of awareness itself. To realise our authentic self, we begin with first recognising what is inauthentic, what is unreal, in order to discover the unchanging reality within your own home, your own being.

The starting point is that human beings have much to discover about Being, and not just psychological exploration, as modern western paradigms generally understand but exploring the furtherest reaches of human potential. Western psychology is the product and exponent of European enlightenment and dominated by its outdated colonial and Freudian underpinning.

Gurmat, like Buddhist and Hindu mythos, are rooted in a different matrix, including experiential mapping of mind, body and consciousness. Gurmat, as a theory and practice, is practical and transcendental in nature. Although Gurmat addresses the existential issues from a first person perspective, it is inclusive in approach and does not ignore the mundane concerns of everyday life and social responsibility and welfare.

In contrast to the purely intellectual approach, the Bhakti movement dominated India during 15-16th century.) It is during this time the Sikh spiritual tradition emerged in Northern India when, the first Sikh Guru, Guru Nanak, declared: There is no Hindu and no Muslim, there is only the One sacred essence within all. Sikhi is regarded as Prem bhakti marg (path of egoloss or love) and focuses on improving life for oneself, and enable the betterment of society and its' service.

Gurmat is firmly founded on Bhakti and Raj yoga. Their practice leads to a gradual transformation of the emotional life of the seeker, such that the seeker ultimately resides in a state of pure and unconditional love of, and for the sacred rooted within oneself and yet expressed with all.

Bhakti is the transformation process in emotional states of the aspirant, from self-oriented states, (survival/pleasure/ ego orientation), to major states of mergence, unity and joy (love orientation).

Bhakti involves the transformation of the emotional states, influencing both the Rasa and the bhavuna. Rasa being the initial stimulus accessed through senses, leading to the bhavuna, the felt experience. In Bhakti, these states can be accessed through a range of contemplative practices such as transcendental meditation, breath, sound meditation, mantra meditations, chanting, singing and through selfless service or sewa. Through such practices the seeker gradually experiences a dissolution of their ego self, transcending their everyday mundane experience and experience the emotion resulting from the loss of a separate sense of "I"-amness or "mine" into a state of pure and absolute universal love, sweetness and appreciation.

The process of transformation is a gradual development towards optimum psycho-spiritual health and wellbeing. Wellbeing, "tand rusti" or "swastha" is being rooted in the Self as awareness, beyond the ego-self. The self here is the deeper or higher self, our innate essential awareness and individual identity, beyond the layers of our body, thoughts, emotions and sensations.

Bhakti movement differs from the Buddhist and Hindu psychological models. All Buddhist schools employ meditation but some add more specific yogic practices, like Pranayama and Mantra with little or no focus on engagement within life, family and society. Gurmat focuses both internally through meditation, mantras and wisdom teaching, but also, externally, through actions in society, as householder, engaged in ethical work and selfless service.

Consciousness – Nature of reality: Gurmat (cit, cheytanya) and Western Perspectives on Consciousness

Western psychology has its roots in the 17th century philosophers, such as Rene Descartes, his famous statement "I think, therefore I am" (Descartes *Principia Philosophiae*) gives rise to a dualistic worldview, which is the current western paradigm. His thesis is that the mind and body are distinct and separate, known as the "mind-body dualism." He concluded that the nature of the mind (limited to only the thinking fuction, non-extended thing) is completely different from that of the body (an extended, non-thinking thing), and therefore it is possible for one to exist without the other. There is no consideration or comprehension of consciousness within this model, which to this day dominates western psychology.[15,16]

Thus, the approach to consciousness by western philosophers and psychologist has been mechanistically and thus they have struggled to comprehend the nature of consciousness or its essential properties, giving rise to an incomplete, confused, incoherent and limited understanding of the nature of consciousness let alone existence itself. This is further confused by considering consciousness is as a by-product of the brain thus dividing mind from body, with little regard for consciousness.

Consciousness has been studied through subjective experience for over 3000 years in Eastern traditions, giving rise to a clear and comprehensive approach to consciousness in terms of psychology, therapy and development of human potential. Quantum physics is now shedding insights into the nature of the manifesting universe and its relationship to consciousness, confirming at many levels the Eastern understanding of the nature of consciousness.

There are fundamental differences between Western and Eastern psychological models in their understanding of consciousness. Neither Western philosophy nor Western psychology *differentiate* Mind from Consciousness nor does there appears to be any clear distinction between 'mind', 'intellect', 'consciousness' or "awareness". In contrast, Gurmat in line with Eastern schools of psychology makes a clear distinction between mind (maan) and consciousness (cit, cheytanya) where the mind (Maan) is considered a very subtle form of matter, while consciousness is noncorporeal. In contrast, western psychology considers the consciousness as a distinctive character of Mind

According to Gurmat, Parmatma is self-illuminated pure consciousness, (cheytanya). This Consciousness is the ground of being, the ultimate reality whose infinite variety of manifestations are the world of phenomena. Akaal Purekh (timeless or eternal Consciousness or Being) is described as the first principle, and is identical with the egoless-self of man, known as Atman.

> Jinee Aatham Cheeniaa Paramaatham Soee II
> Eaeko Anmrith Birakh Hai Fal Anmrith Hoee II6II
> *Those who recognise their own consciouness, are*
> *themselves the Supreme Consciousness.*
> *The One Consciounsess is the tree of ambrosial nectar,*
> *which bears the ambrosial fruit. II6II*
> (Raag Asa Guru Nanak Dev 421)

From this ultimate reality, all phenomena are derived, by it, all are supported, and finally disappear within in, the ceaseless and infinite process of Existence or Ongkaaar.

Existence, is the continuous manifestation as a result of vibrational energies (Shabad) across a spectrum in which light is at one end and matter is its grosser manifestation.

> Initially Ongkar was uttered and from this vibration all Existence manifested."
>
>   (Sri Guru Gobind Singh Ji, Chaubis Avatar, pauri 30)

In Ongkaar alone the apparent differences of the phenomenal world are unified. Phenomena or maya in principle are all objects of Consciousness, subject to the process of creation, growth and destruction, existing in time and space for all material objects, yet only in time for thoughts, emotions, feelings, sensation and dreams.

Akaaal Purekh also known as Braham or Paramatma is Singular, manifest (sargun), unmanifest (no-thingness), emptiness (nirgun), unborn, unchanging, undying, eternal, beyond time, self-illuminating, never was there a time Paramatma did not exist nor will there ever be a time when it will not exist. Although Paramatma is not male or female nor it, but "Tat" the "essence of reality". Within Gurmat, all existence is seen as "feminine" while, Paramatma as "masculine".

Atma, individualised embodied consciousness, spiritual self, like Parmatma, is objectless, unconditioned and pure. This is different from the Jiva, the conditioned dynamic psycho-physiological activity or ego, also known as Hau-mai. The undifferentiated totality of consciousness known as "Maan" (pronounced "mun"), through its interaction with Existence, is conditioned and split into a dynamic and active self-preserving ego which perceives itself as differentiated and separate, with a sense of duality (duja).

At an individual Atma level, Gurmat discerns four states of consciousness: three ordinary states of consciousness, namely waking (jâgrat), dreaming (svapna), and deep sleep (sukhopti), which correspond to the three bodies, namely the gross body (Astool), the subtle body (Suksham), and the causal body (Karan), and a fourth state of consciousness called "Turiya" or "Chautha Paad".

The Atma or consciousness in life is that which experiences gross objects during the waking state, subtle objects during the dream state and the bliss arising from absence of the duality of subject and object in dreamless sleep. The Atma is surrounded by five layers or sheaths known as "koshas" and consciousness is "hidden in the cave" of the sheaths.

The three mundane states of consciousness can be summarised as follows:

"Jågrat" or the first state is the waking state in which one is aware of the day to day life. It is defined by the actions of the mind engaging with the awareness through sensory organs; this is described as outward-knowing. In the waking consciousness, there is a continuous sense of I-am-ness '(Haumai -ego-body complex) and awareness of thoughts, sensations, feelings and so on as objects of consciousness; these are phenomena which rise, are sustained and dissolve, yet, consciousness remains intact and the same.

"Svapna" or the second state is the dreaming mind, when the awareness is entirely identified with the internal psychological apparatus, or "antakaran"; this is described as the inward-knowing, subtle body.

"Sukhopti" or the third state of deep sleep is characterized by the complete absence of "antahkaranvitti" or mental modifications. It is the causal body. This state is one shrouded in ignorance in which there is no conscious awareness of experiencing dreamless sleeping state.

"Turiya" or the fourth state is the release from the ego-bondage and is experienced when "cravings/desire (trisanaa) are extinguished". Guru Nanak in his discourse with the Siddha Yogis states:

"Shunya" is the pervading nirguna Paramatma or Braham as pure consciousness. The three states of consciousness are directly connected with the three bodies. Shunya is the One indescribable formless (nirgun) Absolute in its full effulgence.

> a(n)thar su(n)na(n) baahar su(n)na(n) thribhavan su(n)n masu(n)na(n) ||
> chouthhae su(n)nai jo nar jaanai thaa ko paap n pu(n)na(n) ||
> ghatt ghatt su(n)n kaa jaanai bhaeo || aadh purakh nira(n)jan dhaeo ||
>
> *Shunya within, Shunya without, The absolute Shunya totally fills the three worlds.*
> *One who knows the fourth state is the witness untouched by virtue or vice.*
> *Within each and every thing exists Shunya; That Shunya is the original untainted Paramatma.*
>
> (Guru Nanak Dev Ji, Sidh Gosht, pauri 51)

According to Guru Nanak and Bhai Gurdas, "Turiya" only arises through the Satguru and not through indirect knowledge.

Satguru (Master, authentic teacher) is one who is self-realised and enlightened having transcended the ego bound sense of self through the teaching, practise and compassion of a living master.

Though originated in India, Gurmat is pan human and applicable to all humanity. Gurmat enables one to free themselves from their own self-limiting ego-bound bondages, helps recognise and transcend internal source of suffering and actualise ones full potential. The teachings and experience from a Satguru focuses on the essential nature of one's being and provides a path through which one comes to experience it directly. Satguru enables one to discover their own path and pursue their own path of evolution in a wider time-space framework.

ਸਤਿ ਪੁਰਖੁ ਜਿਨਿ ਜਾਨਿਆ ਸਤਿਗੁਰੁ ਤਿਸ ਕਾ ਨਾਉ ॥
ਤਿਸ ਕੈ ਸੰਗਿ ਸਿਖੁ ਉਧਰੈ ਨਾਨਕ ਹਰਿ ਗੁਨ ਗਾਉ ॥੧॥

Sath Purakh Jin Jaaniaa Sathigur This Kaa Naao ॥
This Kai Sang Sikh Oudhharai Naanak Har Gun Gaao ॥1॥

The one who knows the Pure Consciouness, is known as SatGuru.

In His Company, the Sikh(the learner) is liberated, O Nanak, singing the Glorious Praises of the One. ॥1॥

(Raag Gauri Sukhmanee Guru Arjan Dev Ang:286)

From the awake, dreaming and dreamless sleep, Turiya blossoms forth through the teachings of the Guru.

(Bhai Gurdas Ji, Svaiya 159)

janam marai thrai gun hithakaar ॥
chaarae baedh kathhehi aakaar ॥
theen avasathhaa kehehi vakhiaan ॥
thureeaavasathhaa sathigur thae har jaan ॥1॥

One who is engrossed with the three qualities is subject to birth and death. The four Vedas speak only of the visible forms.

They describe and explain the three states of consciousness,

but the fourth state (turiya), in which Hari is known, is known only through the True Guru. ॥1॥

(Sri Guru Nanak Dev Ji, Rag Gauri p 154)

Turiya is not a state of consciousness as the other three, awake, dream and dreamlessness dual-states, but a non-dual awareness, beyond subject-object as Nirguna (formless), untainted, "unfathomable" and "unperceivable" Pure consciousness experience as a non-dual Oneness-Presence. Only through transcending the three states can the unfathomable be known intuitively.

Jaisae Jal Mehi Kamal Niraalam Muragaaee Nai Saanae ॥
Surath Sabadh Bhav Saagar Thareeai Naanak Naam Vakhaanae ॥

Rehehi Eikaanth Eaeko Man Vasiaa Aasaa Maahi Niraaso ||
Agam Agochar Dhaekh Dhikhaaeae Naanak Thaa Kaa
Dhaaso ||5|

*As the lotus flower floats remains untouched upon the
surface of the water, and the duck swims through the
stream;*
*With awareness focused on the Shabad, one crosses over
the terrifying world-ocean. O'Nanak, chant the Naam.*
*Their minds are singularly immersed in Oneness, free of
expectations*
*They are the ones who see and inspire others to see the
inaccessible, unfathomable One. Nanak is their
slave. ||5||*

(Raag Raamkali Guru Nanak Dev)

"Turiya" is both timeless and space less; it can be
described in various ways depending on one's level of
experience, including increased awareness, tranquillity,
profound peace, unity, unmeasurable happiness, deep
contentment or relaxed alertness.

ਇਕ ਮਨਿ ਏਕੁ ਧਿਆਈਐ ਮਨ ਕੀ ਲਾਹਿ ਭਰਾਂਤਿ ॥

Eik Man Eaek Dhhiaaeeai Man Kee Laahi Bharaanth ||

*With one-pointed mind, meditate on the Oneness, and the
doubts of your mind will be dispelled.*

(Guru Arjan Dev Ang 47)

Introducing key concepts in Gurmat

We begin with the terms Guru and Sikh. Guru consists
of two words, Gu and Ru, gu means darkness or heavy; the
formless, hidden and invisible power of Divinity, while ru
means light, visible beauty and luster of being. Guru is one
who through their direct experience has achieved self-
realization and is thus able move others from darkness or
ignorance, to knowing or light. The guru is more than just the
remover of ignorance through knowledge, practice and

grace, but someone who take on total commitment for complete liberation in this and every other life time.

The Guru as a human being who has transceneded their egoic self, and experienced the transformation and self-realisation are the authentic psycho-spiritual therapist who takes on the profound commitment of the student, which may be lifelong to deliver the student to self-realisation.

Sikh means students and importantly emphasizes an attitude of "don't know or not knowing, wishing to know", an openness to learn through knowledge, perception and experience.

The sacred text called the Sri Guru Granth sahib is the central authority and considered as a living Guru or teacher and the teaching are referred to as Gurmat, the understandings or psychology of the enlightened or self-realized. There are three important and distinct sacred texts within the authentic tradition of the Sikhs, Gurmat is the philosophy underlying Sri Guru Granth sahib, Sri Dasam Granth and Sarbloh Granth.

Gurmat emphasizes the recognition of the actual nature of reality to be of fundamental importance in learning about the value of human life, its development and application. One central function of the Guru is to enable the student, to understand and recognize the essence of Reality for themselves, experientially rather than mere knowledge or worst still, belief. The Guru is the transitional link between the student and experiential knowledge. The Guru communicates the nature of life and enables the safe ego-transformation, growth and transcendence through established contemplative practices which have therapeutic history extending back to thousands of years.

In the context of Gurmat, the Guru is Gurbani. Gurbani are the actual words and teachings unadulterated utterance by the self-realised Gurus, Bhagats and mystics.

The teachings contain the wisdom and the essence of ultimate reality as experienced through Shabd, Mantras and Naam (presence) within the sounds vibrations themselves. Gurbani refers to the words of the Gurus, Bhagats and mystics and each sound is considered to contain its own latent vibration and expression as sacred geometrical space, which in themselves catalyze, contribute and progress the self-transformation process.

Mul Mantra

In the context of human conditioning, Gurmat begins by first introducing the nature of reality through its root mantra, the Mul Mantra. Without the correct view and understanding of Existence, one is unable to walk the path towards self realization safely:

> ik-o^Nkaar sat naam kartaa purakh nirbha-o nirvair akaal moorat ajoonee saibha^N gur parsaad.

Mul mantra is the foundation of Gurmat thought and the experience of Reality, or "Tat", the essence of reality, Existence, sacredness. It was uttered by Guru Nanak Dev ji some five hundred and fifty years ago and represents the fundamental nature of Existence, Ultimate reality, or Truth both as at a personal subjective experiential level of here and now, but also at a transcendental level. Mul Mantra defines the reality which can be subjectively verified through the contemplative practices and ethical lifestyle.

Only through our experience of our immediate reality, are we able to experience ultimate Reality. The Mul Mantra describes both a subjective and objective reality and should not be considered in dualistic terms which describes "God". Mul Mantra is the experience of Existence and thus life, which itself is "Godliness" or sacred and our way of life becomes the "prayer". In other words, life is "God" and living is the "prayer".

Mul mantra describes both the objective observable reality and subjective expereintial reality. The Mul mantra opens the gateway to a truly transformational and transpersonal experience when one engages with it from a non dualistic perspective. Ongkaar is the vibration description of the **continuous process** of creation, preservation, destruction and rebirth infinitum. The Absolute reality is one and non-dual, manifesting itself, through desire, "I am only one — may I become many." This is the primal cause of creation through an unstruck vibration which eventually manifests as sound (struck vibration), and this sound is Om or Ong (pronounced AUM). Through this primal sound vibration Existence manifests as self-aware infinite continuum, the unfolding moment of now.

> ik-o^Nkaar sat naam kartaa purakh nirbha-o nirvair akaal
> moorat ajoonee saibha^N gur parsaad.

1 – One ultimate reality without a second, omnipresent, omnipotent and omniscient presence within which all existence is contained. Eternal Now and here

OnKaar –Entirety of existence as a process of creation, growth, destruction, recreation – a sacred continuum expressed as constant changing of states of birth, growth, death and rebirth

This primal sound Ongkaaar represents the four states of all manifested creation, creating, preserving, destroying and re-creating. This applies to both those which manifests in time, such as thoughts just as much all that manifests in time and space, including the Universe itself.

Ongkaaar also represents the four states of the Consciousness. The three sounds in Om (A-U-M) represent the waking (jagrat), dream (swapna), unconsciousness or dreamless sleep (sushupti) states and the fourth state, Turiya is the silence within which all three states are also contained.Turiya or Chautha Pad (fourth state) is the non-dual, pure consciousness experience of Anand, an ecstatic, joyful, and serene.

> Thrai Gun Maaeiaa Mohu Hai Guramukh Chouthhaa Padh Paae II
>
> *The three qualities hold people in attachment to Maya. The Gurmukh attains the fourth state of higher conscious-ness.*

(Guru Amar Das SGGS 30)

The sound of AUM is also called Pranava, meaning that it sustains life and runs through Prana or breath .

Sat – From the Sanskrit Satya=unchanging, truth, being, existence-consciousness (That which does NOT change)

Naam – Presence as existence, Presence

Satnam – unchanging Presence as the eternal now and here

Kartaa-Purkh – Creativity or Creator within Creation, personified, contained within all that is created, connecting all that ever was created, and all that ever will be created, experientially grounded "here".

Purkh - Consciousness; essential being supporting the play of Kudrat *(Self-creating nature)*; a Consciousness—Knowing, Conscient—beingness, witness, knower, enjoyer, upholder and source of sanction for Nature's unfolding and expression.

Nirbhai – Fearlessness. Fear is anticipation of loss projected into the future, thus fear required a future as a reference point. Fear is unable to exist in the moment of now, although it can be felt in this moment through thoughts of a future event. Fear is the absence of Love

Nirvair – Without hate or enmity, hate requires a past reference point, an event that occurred in ones past that allows us to create thoughts that give rise to feelings of conflict. Feeling or expression of deep-seated ill will.

Akaal – timelessness – Present moment is not a "Time-bound" experience, but a timelessness presence

Moorat – Form, the fullness of all that is seen, experienced and felt.

Ajoone – beyond birth, without birth, how can the present moment be born?

Saibhang – self-existent, that which exists from its self, a fractal in nature

Gur – awareness, shifting from non-knowing to knowing

Parshaad – overcoming ignorance, knowing, grace, "sweetness", safety and security

GurParshaad – The experience of "Presence" is grace

ਤਤੈ ਸਾਰ ਨ ਜਾਣੀ ਗੁਰੂ ਬਾਝਹੁ ਤਤੈ ਸਾਰ ਨ ਜਾਣੀ ॥

Thathai Saar N Jaanee Guroo Baajhahu Thathai Saar N Jaanee ||

They do not know the true essence of reality without the Guru; they do not know the true essence of reality.
(Raag Raamkali Guru Amar Das Ang:920)

Ones' subjective understanding of reality directly impacts one's psychology, mentality and physiology.

In other words, a distorted worldview gives rise to misunderstanding of reality will inevitably influence one's engagement with life, self-image, self-esteem and outcome.

The distorted worldview leads us to believe "objective reality" to be permanent and remains the "same", and taking sense of self for granted. Such beliefs inevitably lead to distress and suffering upon the discovery of an essential truth about the nature of reality, in which everything changes and nothing remains. Thus attachment to youth and effort to maintain youth will inevitably lead to distresses as one experience the signs of aging, to the point, where people will have surgery performed to try and maintain that which is changing, an obvious state of mental turmoil and anguish.

> Ik Oankaar Sathigur Prasaadh II
>
> Kaachee Dhaeh Moh Fun Baandhhee Sath Kathor Kucheel
>   Kugiaanee II
>
> Dhhaavath Bhramath Rehan Nehee Paavath Paarabreham
>   Kee Gath Nehee Jaanee II
>
> Joban Roop Maaeiaa Madh Maathaa Bicharath Bikal
>   Badda Abhimaanee II
>
> *One Universal Creator, sustainer, destroyer, by the grace*
>   *of authentic Guru*
>
> *This body is frail and transitory, and bound to emotional*
>   *attachment. I am foolish, stone-hearted, filthy and*
>   *unwise.*
>
> *My mind wanders and wobbles, and will not hold steady.*
>   *It does not know the state of the Supreme Oneness.*
>
> *I am intoxicated with the wine of youth, beauty and the*
>   *riches of Maya.*
>
> *I wander around perplexed, in excessive egotistical pride.*
>   (Savaiye Guru Arjan Dev Ang:1387)

> Dhhan Joban Ar Fularraa Naatheearrae Dhin Chaar II
>
> Paban Kaerae Path Jio Dtal Dtul Junmanehaar II1II
>
> *Wealth, the beauty of youth and flowers are guests for only*
>   *a few days.*
>
> *Like the leaves of the water-lily, they wither and fade and*
>   *finally die. II1II*
>
>   (Sri Raag Guru Nanak Dev Ang:23)

Ik- Oneness

Ik – 1 not two.

What Gurmat has been asserting for over 500 years, only now are scientists beginning to accept that everything in existence is a form of vibration, a continuous pulsating, a singular interconnected Universe(s).

Gurmat asserts Ongkaar (Aum) the only one, singular

ultimate reality which includes everything manifesting and expressing itself as an interconnected, interdependent duality. The singularity manifests as a vibration or waves, which at their fundamental level is considered within Gurmat as the sound ONG (variation of AUM) giving rise to all Existence.

Ongkaar describes the unfolding and cyclic nature of Existence, from creation, growth, destruction and re-creation repeated infinitum with all Existence and as Existence itself known as Kudharat.

From this perspective, there is no difference between "you" and "other", and in fact, "You" are in "God", and "God" is "you", we are born in it, live in it and die it, there is no other

ਨਿਰੰਕਾਰ ਆਕਾਰ ਆਪਿ ਨਿਰਗੁਨ ਸਰਗੁਨ ਏਕ ॥
ਏਕਹਿ ਏਕ ਬਖਾਨਨੋ ਨਾਨਕ ਏਕ ਅਨੇਕ ॥੧॥

Nirankaar Aakaar Aap Niragun Saragun Eaek ॥~
Eaekehi Eaek Bakhaanano Naanak Eaek Anaek ॥1॥
Formless and form One without attributes and with attributes
Describe the Oneness as One, and Only One; O Nanak,
One is one, yet the many. ॥1॥

(Raag Gauri Guru Arjan Dev Ang:250

Ik (Oneness) Ongkaar (also called Brahman expanding Existence) is the ultimate reality, whose various manifesting forms, is the world of phenomena and expressed through the underlying vibration in all existence, Ongkaar, playing out the process of creation, growth, destruction and re-creation. Ik is the fundamental reality underlying all objects and experiences. Consciousness is not a property of Ik or Brahman, but its very nature; never was there a time without Ik nor will there ever be a time without Ik. This Oneness is ultimate reality, without a second, unborn, uncreated, beyond the confines of time, undying, self-creating and eternal.

Brahman is both Nirguna, without attributes and formless-
ness, yet it is also Sarguna, all form. Non-duality is the
Mother of all Existence and the underlying fabric of all
manifestation.

Brahman cannot be known objectively, distinct from
oneself, but can be experienced directly in the world of
changing forms and shapes (sarguna) through self-realisation
(atam gyan).

ਅਚਰਜ ਕਥਾ ਮਹਾ ਅਨੂਪ ॥
ਪ੍ਰਾਤਮਾ ਪਾਰਬ੍ਰਹਮ ਕਾ ਰੂਪ ॥ਰਹਾਉ॥

Acharaj Kaththaa Mehaa Anoop ||
Praathamaa Paarabreham Kaa Roop || Rehaao ||
This description is wondrous and incomparable
The very form of the Atma (individualized consciousness)
is Parbraham ||Pause||

(Raag Gond Guru Arjan Dev 868)

The appearance of plurality or duality is as a result of
natural state of ignorance (*avidya*), inherent as the ego-
complex develops. The world of experience is neither real
nor unreal; real as it's experienced, unreal as its temporary.

This reality is obscured by a mental veil, or Hau, our
conditioned sense of self, the psychological construct of "I"
am, which is essential for human function but also becomes
the barrier and boundary preventing the fulfilment of human
potential beyond this ego-complex.

ਚੁਕਾ ਪੜਦਾ ਤਾਂ ਨਦਰੀ ਆਇਆ ॥

Chookaa Parradhaa Thaan Nadharee Aaeiaa ||
When the veil of illusion is removed, then I come to see
You.

(Raag Bhaira-o: Guru Arjan Dev. Ang 1141)

ਮਨਮੁਖਿ ਹਉਮੈ ਵਿਛੁੜੇ ਮੇਰੀ ਜਿੰਦੁੜੀਏ ਬਿਖੁ ਬਾਧੇ ਹਉਮੈ ਜਾਲੇ ਰਾਮ ॥

Manamukh Houmai Vishhurrae Maeree Jindhurreeeae
Bikh Baadhhae Houmai Jaalae Raam ||

Manmukh (those fused to the content of their mind) are separated by their ego, O my soul; bound to poison, the ego burn (creates suffering).

(Ang 538 Line 17 Raag Bihaagrhaa: Guru Ram Das)

The removal of the illusion of duality and separateness experienced as an absence of one's sense of separateness facilitates our mental, emotional and spiritual health and wellbeing.

ਹਉਮੈ ਦੁਬਿਧਾ ਬਿਨਸਿ ਜਾਇ ਸਹਜੇ ਸੁਖਿ ਸਮਾਈਐ ॥

Houmai Dhubidhhaa Binas Jaae Sehajae Sukh Samaaeeai II

(Raag Gauri Bairaagan: Guru Amar Das Ang 163 Line 2)

When egotism and duality are eradicated, one harmoniously merges in peace.

ਗੁਰਮੁਖਿ ਮੇਲੇ ਆਪੁ ਗਵਾਏ ॥

Guramukh (mindfully aware) Maelae Aap Gavaaeae II

The Gurmukhs shed their ego and merge.3.

(Ang 232 Line 18 Raag Gauri: Guru Amar Das)

Existence can be considered to be an ocean, while all manifestation within existence are the "ice-cubes" floating in this ocean, made on water and in water. This non-dual worldview has implications on our self-image, self-esteem, responsibilities and engagement in life as highlighted below.

In a non-dual state of consciousness, the experience of opposites disappear. In non-dual states of consciousness, duality—as it is experienced in relative existence—disappears, and one enter a great sense of centered awareness and serenity, awareness per se.

It is important to realize that non-dual states of consciousness are relative to the perceiver. Thus, if one experiences non-duality through the heart chakra, one experiences impersonal love together with a deep sense of

cosmic connection, where one becomes the "beloved" as
everything else is that witnessed.

ਗੁਰ ਮਿਲਿਐ ਨਾਮੁ ਪਾਈਐ ਚੁਕੈ ਮੋਹ ਪਿਆਸ ॥
ਹਰਿ ਸੇਤੀ ਮਨੁ ਰਵਿ ਰਹਿਆ ਘਰ ਹੀ ਮਾਹਿ ਉਦਾਸੁ ॥

Gur Miliai Naam Paaeeai Chookai Moh Piaas II
Har Saethee Man Rav Rehiaa Ghar Hee Maahi Oudhaas II

*Meeting with the Guru, the Naam is obtained, and the thirst
of emotional attachment departs.*
*When the mind is permeated with Oneness, one remains
detached within the home of the heart.*

(Raag Guru Amar Das)

Duality – dubda

Gurmat is firmly nondual in its worldview. Nondualism
in terms of psychology refers to unified consciousness,
primordial, natural awareness without subject or object duality,
known as "turiya".

Every form including compounds, molecules, atoms,
right down to sub atomic particles and beyond confirms
that, everything is vibrating. This vibration is found in all
manifestation, and is the single sound Ong (Aum or Om), the
sacred source of all existence.

In human experience, the first and foremost duality is
that of the subject and object, everything contains this
duality, the seer and the seen, no hearing without the hearer,
and so on. Both subject and object serve as the ground for
each other, without object there is no subject, and without
subject there can be no object. As the mind is conditioned
to identify with its psychophysical or mind/body as an entity,
it separates and creates its sense of self or Haumai.

This is a shift of our perception from self-unconscious-
ness into a self-conscious separate individuality, bound in
the duality of subject and object. Our subjective point-of-view
is our subjective experience of duality.

Gurmat teaches the integration of duality, as it is the one non-dual consciousness, which manifests itself as a dual, contrasting manifestation of opposites. This world described in opposites creates a sense of insecurity, which catalyses the formation of attachments in order to provide a sense of security.

Duality as Shiv and Shakti is the very play of existence, Kurdat (nature/existence), the fundamental vibration, alternating changes form and shapes is eternal. Existence manifests itself as a fractal, creating itself, from itself. Ik Ongkaar or Oneness consists of that which is formless, masculine, passive, transcendent, eternal principle as Shiva, and the manifesting feminine form, active, immanent, temporal principle as Shakti.

> Jeh Dhaekhaa Theh Rav Rehae Siv Sakathee Kaa Mael ॥
>
> *Wherever I look, I see the Onenesspervading there, in the union of shiva and shakti, of consciousness and matter.*
>
> (Sri Raag: Guru Nanak Dev Ang 21)

It is an essential component towards unification and non-dual experience, for only through the cultivation of one's sense of separated self and its development, does one arrive through own individuality, temporary existence and vulnerability, and progressively through the Naam Symran arrive at a sense of wholeness and unity, "mool roop", essential or root form.

> Prathhamae Thiaagee Houmai Preeth ॥
> Dhutheeaa Thiaagee Logaa Reeth ॥
> Thrai Gun Thiaag Dhurajan Meeth Samaanae ॥
> Thureeaa Gun Mil Saadhh Pashhaanae ॥2॥
>
> *First, I renounced my egotistical love of myself.*
> *Second, I renounced the ways of the world.*

Renouncing the three qualities, I look alike upon friend and
*   enemy.*
And then, the fourth state of non-duality was revealed to
*   me by the Holy One. ||2||*

(Raag Asa Guru Arjan Dev 370)x

Gourree Bairaagan Mehalaa 3 ||
Sathigur Thae Giaan Paaeiaa Har Thath Beechaaraa ||
Math Maleen Paragatt Bhee Jap Naam Muraaraa ||
Siv Sakath Mittaaeeaa Chookaa Andhhiaaraa ||
Gauree Bairaagan, Third Mehl:
From the True Guru, I obtained spiritual wisdom; I
*   contemplate the essence of Oneness.*
My polluted intellect was enlightened by chanting Naam.
The distinction between Shiva and Shakti - mind and matter -
*   has been destroyed, and the darkness has been dispelled.*

(Guru Amar Das Ang:163)

Through Symran (right mindfulness awareness of Experience in the present moment), awareness progressively matures and the sense of duality is shed, giving rise to the nondual experience of pure consciousness or Naam.

Symran practises enable one to access ever deepening experiential insights one of which facilitate clarity and equanimity. This changes our perception of the manifesting world and life experience beyond duality towards the realisation of interconnectedness, interdependence and singularity.

Eaek Acharaj Jan Dhaekhahu Bhaaee ||
Dhubidhhaa Maar Har Mann Vasaaee ||
Naam Amolak N Paaeiaa Jaae ||
Gur Parasaadh Vasai Man Aae ||3||
O my humble Siblings of Destiny, behold this strange and
*   wonderful thing:*
Duality is overcome, and One dwells within the mind.
Naam is priceless; it cannot be taken.
By Guru's Grace, it comes to abide in the mind. ||3|

(Raag Dhanaasree Guru Amar Das Ang:663)

Aap Karathaa Aap Bhugathaa Aap Sagal Beechaareeaa ||
One Creator (Object), One enjoyer (Subject); One
Contemplator of all (experience).

(Guru Nanak Dev 765)

Jeh Dhaekhaa Theh Eaek Thoon Sathigur Dheeaa
Dhikhaae ||
*Wherever I look, I see only you. The True Guru has
inspired me to see you.*

(Guru Nanak Dev 55)

Hukam – The Divine balancing imperative

The literal meaning of Hukam is command or divine
command; In Gurmat, the issuer of the command
(Unchanging consciousness in non-dual joy) is not separated
from the command itself. In other words, the commander
and the command are the same. Hukam is an ever-evolving
manifestation of the now. Hukam categorically presupposes
and implies a direction and a goal in its creative movement.
Hukam is synonymous with Naam or Presence (discussed
later)

Hukam is the holistic universal principle of continuous
cyclic states of change underlying all existence, from the
creation of universes to the interactions in everyday living.
This imperative universal law is inscribed within Existence
and is expressed as the continuous moment by moment
unfolding of all creation. It is as a result of Hukam one takes
birth, Hukam is the process of creation, growth, death and
re-birth. The experience of "time" is the unfolding Hukam.
Hukam itself cannot be described, yet can be directly
experienced and realized.

Hukam is the process of evolution, of becoming,
evolving together in an interconnected undivided wholeness.

ਹੁਕਮੈ ਅੰਦਰਿ ਸਭੁ ਕੋ ਬਾਹਰਿ ਹੁਕਮ ਨ ਕੋਇ ॥

hukamai Andhar Sabh Ko Baahar hukam N Koe ||

Everything is subject toHukam; nothing is beyond Hukam.
(Guru Nanak Dev SGGS 1)

ਹੁਕਮੇ ਆਇਆ ਹੁਕਮਿ ਸਮਾਇਆ ॥
ਹੁਕਮੇ ਦੀਸੈ ਜਗਤੁ ਉਪਾਇਆ ॥
ਹੁਕਮੇ ਸੁਰਗੁ ਮਛੁ ਪਇਆਲਾ ਹੁਕਮੇ ਕਲਾ ਰਹਾਇਦਾ ॥੧੦॥
ਹੁਕਮੇ ਧਰਤੀ ਧਉਲ ਸਿਰਿ ਭਾਰੰ ॥
ਹੁਕਮੇ ਪਉਣ ਪਾਣੀ ਗੈਨਾਰੰ ॥
ਹੁਕਮੇ ਸਿਵ ਸਕਤੀ ਘਰਿ ਵਾਸਾ ਹੁਕਮੇ ਖੇਲ ਖੇਲਾਇਦਾ ॥੧੧॥
ਹੁਕਮੇ ਆਡਾਣੇ ਆਗਾਸੀ ॥
ਹੁਕਮੇ ਜਲ ਥਲ ਤ੍ਰਿਭਵਣ ਵਾਸੀ ॥
ਹੁਕਮੇ ਸਾਸ ਗਿਰਾਸ ਸਦਾ ਫੁਨਿ ਹੁਕਮੇ ਦੇਖਿ ਦਿਖਾਇਦਾ ॥੧੨॥

Hukamae Aaeiaa Hukam Samaaeiaa ||

Hukamae Dheesai Jagath Oupaaeiaa ||

Hukamae Surag Mashh Paeiaalaa Hukamae Kalaa
    Rehaaeidhaa ||10||

Hukamae Dhharathee Dhhoul Sir Bhaaran ||

Hukamae Poun Paanee Gainaaran ||

Hukamae Siv Sakathee Ghar Vaasaa Hukamae Khael
    Khaelaaeidhaa ||11||

Hukamae aadhaane aagaasee ||

Hukamae Jal Thhal Thribhavan Vaasee ||

Hukamae Saas Giraas Sadhaa Fun Hukamae Dhaekh
    Dhikhaaeidhaa ||12||

*Through Hukam one come, through Hukam one merge
    into Existence again.*
Through Hukam Existence is formed.
*Through Hukam the heavens, universes and nether
    regions are created; Hukam supports them. ||10||*
*Hukam is the mythical bull which supports the burden of
    the earth on its head.*
Through Hukam air, water and fire came into being.
*Through hukam one dwells in the house of matter and
    energy - Shiva and Shakti.*
Through Hukam, this play is played. ||11||

Through Hukam space is abound
Through Hukam life dwell in the water,land and througi iout
the three worlds.
Through Hukam we draw our breath and receive our food;
Through hukam we are taken care of and inspired to
see. ||12||

(Raag Maaroo Guru Nanak Dev Ang:1037)

One important aspect of reality ("Tat" = suchness or existence) according to Gurmat is impermanence the constant process of change through creation, growth, destruction and, recreation as endless cycles within cycles binding all existence, including human beings within one unchanging wholeness or ultimate reality.

ਪੇਖੁ ਹਰਿਚੰਦਉਰੜੀ ਅਸਥਿਰੁ ਕਿਛੁ ਨਾਹੀ ॥

Paekh Harichandhourarree Asathhir Kishh Naahee ||
Behold - the world is a mirage; nothing here is permanent.
(Guru Arjan Dev.Ang 461)

Impermanence or change is the essential characteristic of all phenomenal existence, a continuous process happening in the moment of now. Not recognizing the changing and impermanent nature of reality is a central feature of psychological suffering. Attachment to ideas, thoughts, objects, people, relationships and life itself lead to sufferings, while recognizing the changing nature of existence and cultivating non-attachment provides one with the keys towards inner peace and contentment.

Non acceptance and resistance to "the way things are" is the root cause of psychological suffering, and by recognizing, understanding and accepting the nature of reality, particularly impermanency, leads to a less resistant attitude and experiences, where one develops the ability to see things for how they are and move towards less psychological suffering.

ਸਭੁ ਇਕੋ ਹੁਕਮੁ ਵਰਤਦਾ ਮੰਨਿਐ ਸੁਖੁ ਪਾਈ ॥੩॥

Sabh Eiko hukam Varathadhaa Manniai Sukh
    Paaee ॥3॥

*The One hukam is all-pervasive accepting it one finds
    peace. ॥3॥*

(Guru Amar Das Ang 948)

ਗੁਰਮੁਖਿ ਹੋਇ ਸੁ ਹੁਕਮੁ ਪਛਾਣੈ ਮਾਨੈ ਹੁਕਮੁ ਸਮਾਇਦਾ ॥੯॥

Guramukh Hoe S hukam Pashhaanai Maanai hukam
    Samaaeidhaa ॥9॥

*One who becomes gurmukh realizes the hukam, through
    its acceptancemerges (two becomes one). ॥9॥*

(Guru Nanak Dev Ang 1037)

The self-realized or Gurmukhs, are attuned to cycles of
change, with awareness of their temporary place in the web
of existence and act accordingly, without the need to grasp
at every pleasant experience and avoid every unpleasant
experience.

Gourree Mehalaa 5 ॥
Jaa Kai Dhukh Sukh Sam Kar Jaapai ॥
Thaa Ko Kaarraa Kehaa Biaapai ॥1॥
Gauree, Fifth Mehl:
*Those who look alike upon pleasure and pain how can
    anxiety touch them? ॥1॥*

(Raag Gauri Guru Arjan Dev Ang:186 Line: 12)

pourree ॥
mamaa jaahoo maram pashhaanaa ॥
bhaettath saadhhasa(n)g patheeaanaa ॥
dhukh sukh ouaa kai samath beechaaraa ॥
narak surag rehath aouthaaraa ॥
thaahoo sa(n)g thaahoo niralaepaa ॥
pooran ghatt ghatt purakh bisaekhaa ॥
ouaa ras mehi ouaahoo sukh paaeiaa ॥
naanak lipath nehee thih maaeiaa ॥42॥

Pauree:

MAMMA: Those who understand Existences mystery are satisfied, joining the Saadh Sangat (company of self-realised), the Company of the Holy.

They look upon pleasure and pain as the same.

They are exempt from incarnation into heaven or hell.

They live in the world, and yet they are detached from it.

The Sublime Lord, the Primal Being, is totally pervading each and every heart.

In His Love, they find peace.

O Nanak, Maya does not cling to them at all. ||42||

Recognizing Hukam as the continuous process, which is responsible for all forms, all creation, growth, destruction, for pleasure and suffering, for life and all its processes, and for inspiring one to discover and recognize it for what it is, helps dissolve our ego, sense of separation.

ਹੁਕਮੈ ਬੂਝੈ ਤਤੁ ਪਛਾਣੈ ॥

Hukamai Boojhai Thath Pashhaanai ||

Whoever understands the Hukam realizes the essence of reality.

(Raag Malar Guru Nanak Dev Ang:1289)

ਹੁਕਮੈ ਅੰਦਰਿ ਸਭੁ ਕੋ ਬਾਹਰਿ ਹੁਕਮ ਨ ਕੋਇ ॥
ਨਾਨਕ ਹੁਕਮੈ ਜੇ ਬੁਝੈ ਤ ਹਉਮੈ ਕਹੈ ਨ ਕੋਇ ॥੨॥

Hukamai Andhar Sabh Ko Baahar Hukam N Koe ||
Naanak Hukamai Jae Bujhai Th Houmai Kehai N Koe ||2||

Everyone is subject to His Command; no one is beyond His Command.

O Nanak, one who understands His Command, does not speak in ego. ||2||

(Jap Guru Nanak Dev Ang:1)

Hukam is the organic ever-evolving manifestation of the now. Through cultivating awareness of the present moment unfolding enables the recognition of hukam, impermanence and finally liberation from both attachments and ego.

Kudhrath – Manifesting creativity

Gurmat considers that the "Creator" which is also the preserver and destroyer (*sat kartar*) and its energy aspect (*Kudrat*) as one, not two separable entities. The energy aspect of the One consciousness involves itself in the affairs of the universe through the agents of creation, preservation, destruction and re-creation; Consciousness is the ground of being is within all creation.

> kudrat kar kai vasi-aa so-ay.
> *He created the Creative Power of the Universe, within which He dwells*
>
> (p 83)

Another important area that needs consideration is the term "lila" or manifested creation as a play within Gurmat. The creative evolution is the manifestation of the creator, or its lila, an act of self expression of the One. Therefore, Existence is not an "illusion", but certainly impermanent and transient, unlike Consciousness itself. The energy aspect of the One is a principle of manifestation, involution and evolution of the universe.

> khin meh thaap uthaapanhaaray kudrat keem na pahee. ||2||7||
> *In an instant, You establish and disestablish; the value of Your Almighty Creative Power cannot be estimated*
>
> (p 529)

The mind is easily conditioned to attach itself to the manifesting creation, or "Maya". Maya is a Sanskrit word which literally means "that which is not" - "ma" means "not", "ya" means "that". The mind attaches itself to that which never ends, yet never exists! The Gurbani defines Maya as follows:

> raag sorat(h) baanee bhagath ravidhaas jee kee
> ik oa(n)kaar sathigur prasaadh ||

jab ham hothae thab thoo naahee ab thoohee mai
naahee ||

anal agam jaisae lehar mae oudhadhh jal kaeval jal
maa(n)hee ||1||

maadhhavae kiaa keheeai bhram aisaa ||

jaisaa maaneeai hoe n thaisaa ||1|| rehaao ||

Raag Sorat'h, The Word Of Devotee Ravi Daas Jee:
One Ongkaar. By The Grace Of The True Guru:
When I am in my ego, then You are not with me. Now that
You are with me, there is no egotism within me.
The wind may raise up huge waves in the vast ocean, but
they are just water in water. ||1||
O Lord, what can I say about such an illusion?
Things are not as they seem. ||1||Pause||

(SGGS 657).

Parameshar (Oneness) is thelimitless Shakti or energy
that can be divided into two groups (1) Spiritual energy; (2)
and material energy or Maya. Hence Maya is not separate
or different than the Supreme Oneness, but its inherent
power, which is responsible for the rising of mirage-like
phenomenal world of names, forms, time and space.

Gurmat consider "Maya" as self-deception in terms of
one's psychological relationship through emotional attachment with existence/creation which arises because of
haumai (ego-complex).

haumai maar sadaa sukh paa-i-aa maa-i-aa moh
chukaavani-aa. ||1||

Subduing your ego, you shall find a lasting peace, and
your emotional attachment to Maya will be dispelled.

(p110)

mohi mohi-aa jaanai door hai.

Infatuated with emotional attachment, they think the One
is far away

(p 210)

Maya is the semi hypnotic mental state that makes one

forget their own essence, giving rise to emotional attachment and creating duality where there is none. Maya, the ever-changing creation from thoughts to the universes are all composed of three qualities, known as the Gunas. The three qualities or 3 Gunas - Saatav (Essense), Raajas (activity/ motion), and Taamas (inertia) are intertwined like threads in a rope that give rise to the world of phenomenon. (Discussed later)

Gurmat experiences the One as Absolute Purusa, Consciouness, the matrix of Creation. The Creator is manifest in all its creation. This Creation is not separate and independent of purusa, but rather an emanation of this purusa called Kudrat (that which is under the power and authority of its creator).

> khaalik khalak khalak meh khaalik poor rahi-o sarab thaaN-ee. ||1|| rahaa-o.
>
> *The Creation is in the Creator, and the Creator is in the Creation, totally pervading and permeating all places.*
> (p 1394)

Such understanding presents far reaching implications in terms of the relationship the between humanity and the creation it exists within. It is within this context a follower of the Gurmat path undergoes transpersonal psychological changes shifting from being attached to the content and structure within our mind, to being identified with awareness or Gur. An evolution from Manmukh (mind facing) to Gurmukh (Gur, that which enlightens, awareness, facing).

Kirpa nadar, prasad, mihar–Abundance

The gurmat worldview considers existence as an ever-flowing abundant resource, which has met the needs of all its forms since the beginning of time, now and forevermore.

Grace is the single most important element in achieving the ultimate state of sahej or optium psycho-spiritual health and wellbeing. Kirpa implies Divine grace that is central to Sikh worldview affirming its trust in a Transcendental Being responsive to the needs of its manifesting creation.

Entire existence is over flowing with grace, it is experienced during states of non doing, by simply being receptive, open. However, due to our identification with the content of our mind, our false sense of self, which creates a barrier and blockage, in recognising and accessing the ever flowing abundance or grace.

Two major barriers to grace are, firstly, whatsoever one does becomes a food for the ego; secondly, whatsoever one does leads them into the "future", and not here and now.

The experience of grace requires one to be here and now, and not be the ego, allowing one to open and whenever one is open the grace is already flowing; it has been flowing forever.

It is through grace one comes across a Satguru, a master, self-realised and enlightened. Through the Satgurus' grace, the disciple recognises the unfolding present moment or Hukam. It is through recognition and merging with hukam, once is graced to transcend the ego-complex. Kirpa is the unconditional compassionate nature of Existence, experienced as "being".

ਗੁਰ ਕਿਰਪਾ ਤੇ ਹੁਕਮੁ ਪਛਾਣੈ ॥
Gur Kirapaa Thae Hukam Pashhaanai ||
Through the grace of a Guru one recognises Hukam
(Guru Nanak Dev 1027)

salok ma 2 ||
akhee baajhahu vaekhanaa vin ka(n)naa sunanaa ||
pairaa baajhahu chalanaa vin hathhaa karanaa ||
jeebhai baajhahu bolanaa eio jeevath maranaa ||
naanak hukam pashhaan kai tho khasamai milanaa ||1||

Salok, Second Mehla:
To see without eyes; to hear without ears;
to walk without feet; to work without hands;
*to speak without a tongue-like this, one remains dead
while yet alive.*
*O Nanak, recognize the Hukam, one merges with the
Master of Existence. ||1||*

(Guru Angad Dev Ji 139)

Suffering is grace as it leads one to recognize the cause of suffering and discover a way to transcend suffering itself.

Naam

Naam – The concept of Naam is central to the Sikh worldview. Naam has a distinct meaning other than simply 'Name'. Naam is a non-dual experience which is both transcendental yet also immanent, Naam is an ontological essence of reality, denoting Divine presence, unchanging Truth, timeless consciousness. Naam refers to the bridge between the invisible, infinite Divinity and its gross manifestation.

Naam is "God", "Akal-Purekh" (timeless consciousness), Naam is the expression and presence of "God" in its creation. Naam is Ultimate Reality itself. *Naam* is that Omnipresent Existence which manifests itself in the form of creation and is the source and sustenance of all beings and things (GG, 284).

Naam is the source of creation pervades all and its manifestation has a structure and order, yet it conforms to a fixed plan. From this point of view *Naam* is identifiable with *hukam*, the divine imperative and divine Grace (*prasad*)

ਏਕੋ ਨਾਮੁ ਹੁਕਮੁ ਹੈ ਨਾਨਕ ਸਤਿਗੁਰਿ ਦੀਆ ਬੁਝਾਇ ਜੀਉ ॥੫॥

Eaeko Naam Hukam Hai Naanak Sathigur Dheeaa Bujhaae Jeeo ||5||

*The One Naam is Hukam; O Nanak, the True Guru has
given me this understanding. ||5 ||*

(Sri Raag Guru Nanak Dev Ang:72)

Naam reflects the immanence of the Transcendent
Oneness in creation. Naam originates from shabd (sound,
words). Shabd are the utterances, the words (bani) of the
Sikh Gurus, mystics and bhagats which communicate Naam
experientially.

From *shabad* has originated *naam*" (GG, 644),

The experience of Naam, Presence is grace, (parshad),
a subjective non-dual experience following ego-
transcendence through the practice of somatic focused
mindfulness awareness with the uninterrupted repetition of
the names of the Divine essence. (Naam Symrann- seeded
meditation). Naam reveals itself once duality is transcended;
an experience which replaces the subjective presence of "I-
am-ness" with Presence.

saacha oupajai saach samaavai saachae soochae eaek
maeiaa ||

jhoot(h)ae aavehi t(h)avar n paavehi dhoojai aavaa goun
bhaeiaa ||

aavaa goun mittai gur sabadhee aapae parakhai bakhas
laeiaa ||

eaekaa baedhan dhoojai biaapee naam rasaaein
veesariaa ||

so boojhai jis aap bujhaaeae gur kai sabadh s mukath
bhaeiaa ||

naanak thaarae thaaranehaaraa houmai dhoojaa
parehariaa ||25||

*We emerge from Truth, and merge into Truth again. The
pure being merges into the unchanging Oneness*

*The false come, and find no place of rest; in duality, they
come and go.*

*This coming and going in reincarnation is ended through
the Word of the Guru's Shabad; Existence itself
analyzes and grants forgiveness.*

> *One who suffers from the disease of duality, forgets the Naam, the source of nectar.*
> *He alone understands, whom the Oneness inspires to understand. Through the Word of the Guru's Shabad, one is liberated.*
> *O Nanak, the Emancipator emancipates one who drives out egotism and duality. ||25||*
> (Guru Nanak Dev Ji in Raag Raamkalee on Pannaa 940)

The goal of Sikh meditation is ego-transcendence through a gradual process of realising and immersing into the sacredness of one's self and thus Existence, union experienced as a non-dual interconnected sovereign sacred Oneness. Sikh practices are geared towards the transformation of the ego-oriented conditioned mind, a continuous active self-attachment or Manmukh, to a non-conditioned sovereign Self or Gurmukh. Manmukh (mind facing) is the "self" attached to itself, in other words, self-fusion with the content of the mind, emotions, sensations, body, desires etc, while Gurmukh (Guru/awareness facing) is self-identification with unchanging witnessing awareness. Sikh meditation practices are focused upon transcending duality towards the experience of Anand or an unbound non-dual Pure Consciousness self or Turiya, a fourth state of consciousness beyond waking, dream and sleep states.

> Thrai Gun Maaeiaa Mohu Hai Guramukh Chouthhaa Padh Paae ||
> *The three qualities hold people in attachment to Maya. The Gurmukh attains the fourth state of higher consciousness.*
> (Sri Raag: Guru Amar Das ang 30)

The choice of meditation practices determines the final state of consciousness achieved, either the path of the Samadhi, where the mind merges with its object, a gradual dissolving of the conditioned ego-self into Self in Union or

Oneness, or, the path towards Nirvana, where the mind takes itself as the object; where all phenomena are finally witnessed to be no-thingness, emptiness; where the drop merges with the Ocean.

Gurmat practice recommends the discipline of Naam Symran (awareness of Presence, awareness of awareness) and Naam Japna (seeded sound based meditation) , Mindfulness Presence, a meditation practice which integrates concentration and insight (veechaar), an interactive combination in which concentration multiplies the effectiveness of insight.

> Saragun Niragun Nirankaar Sunn Samaadhhee Aap ||
> Aapan Keeaa Naanakaa Aapae Hee Fir Jaap ||1||
> *Formless and Form beyond stain, emptiness and Samadhi is One*
> *Manifesting as creation, O Nanak, One meditates on One ||1||*
>
> (Guru Arjan Dev Ji)

Symran is the practice of attuning one's awareness to a Shabad in the form of a Mantra. Shabad here refers to any word considered as a "Mantra". The word "mantra" is composed in Sanskrit of two root words: "Man" means "mind" or "thinking" and "tra" means to "swim across or release or free". Therefore, the meaning of mantra can be defined as that which frees the mind from the bondage of ego.

> Man Rae Sabadh Tharahu Chith Laae ||
> *O mind, swim across, by focusing your consciousness on the Shabad.*
>
> (Guru Nanak Dev 19)

Three types of Mantra are common in Sikh meditation practices: Mool Mantra, Beej Mantra or/and Gur Mantra. The Mool Mantra, root or original mantra consists of 13 words,

Ik-O-an-kaar Satt-e Naamu Kartaa-Purkhu Nir-bhou Nir-vaaeru Akaal-moorat Ajoo-nee Saae-bhan Gur-parsaad.. Beej Mantra, or seed-mantra, is "Ik-Oankar" and "WaheGuru" is the Gur-mantra, a composite mantra from across the four yuga (ages).

> sathijug sathigur vaasadhaev vaavaa vishanaa naam japaavai ||
>
> dhuaapar sathigur hareekrishan haahaa har har naam dhhiaavai ||
>
> thraethae sathigur raam jee raaraa raam japae sukh paavai ||
>
> kalijug naanak gur gobi(n)dh gagaa govi(n)dh naam japaavai ||
>
> chaarae jaagae chahu jugee pa(n)chaaein vich jaae samaavai ||
>
> chaaro(n) ashhar eik kar vaahiguroo jap ma(n)thr japaavai ||
> jehaa(n) thae oupajiaa fir thehaa(n) samaavai ||
>
> (Bhatt Satta and Balwand, 968)

There are a variety of Mantras that can be employed in the practice of Naam Symran. However, the common practice tends to comprise "Waheguru", "Satnaam", "Har", "Hari" and the entire Mul Mantra, the opening formula or the foundational statement.

Authentic Mantra fulfills six conditions.

1. The mantra revealed to a sage or mystic who has then achieved self-realisation throught it and passed it down to others
2. The mantra has a presiding energy
3. The mantra is chanted, recited and sung in a specific meter
4. The mantra possesses a bija, (seed) investing it with an energy that is the essence of the mantra
5. The mantra has dynamic energy (shakti)

6. The mantra is the "plug" that conceals the ᵖ
   consciousness hidden in the mantra. (as soon as the
   plug is removed by constant prolonged repitition and
   listening, pure consciousness is revealed).

The path followed by Guru Nanak and the Sants or
Bhagats is refered to as Bhakti, the essence of which is to
make the object, or "Isth", of one's devotion the central
focus. Bhakti begins on a level of duality, with the practitioner
being separate from the "Isht". However, through gradual
practice, particularly the practice associated with "Prayer of
the Heart" (see below), the practitioner undergoes profound
transformation on all levels of the self towards ego-
transcendence.

The "Isth" or the central authentic authority in Gurmat
meditation practice begins with Shabad or Word. Shabad
according to Guru Nanak is the Guru, (Master, teacher) the
authentic source of self-realisation.

Sabadh Guroo Surath Dhhun Chaelaa ll
The Shabad is the Guru, awareness is the disciple.
(Guru Nanak De Raag Raamkali: Ang 943)

Naam Symran begins with cultivation of Present moment
awareness through right-mindfulness, normally undertaken
sitting upright and beginning with an acknowledgement and
a sense of reverence of what one is about to undertake. The
mind is initially allowed to settle into calmness by focusing
on the flow of the breath at the nostrils and allowing the
breath to breathe itself. Symran combines intention and
attention, intention to hold the focus, attention to the object
of awareness.

Once the mind is settled and calm, this is followed by
Jap.

Jap is the recitation of the mantra at three levels. At the
beginning the repetition of the mantra is aloud. As the

practice matures, the mantra recitation gradually evolves from simple audible verbal recitation to silent verbalization, and, finally, mental repetition or awareness of the presence of the Mantra. Shabd Symran is also practised as Kirtan in the form of chanting and singing, which is normally performed in congregation or "sangat", being in the presence and practicing with those on the path to self-realisation.

The Spiritual evolution or the inner journey has defined stages which begin with "Jap", or recitation, consciously and regularly. Jap can be maintained during life's activity until the mind is gradually occupied with that one singular focal point. Jap matures into Ajaapajap, or the continuous mantra recitation without conscious effort. Ajaapajap over time matures into viraaag, a state of dispassion in which existence is experienced as a constant changing phenomenon, together with a sense of separation from ones' essential sacred nature. Viraaag, gives rise of Ardas, a deep and spontaneously invocation for mergence which culminates into Anand, or non-dual pure consciousness experience.

> Chalath Baisath Sovath Jaagath Gur Manthra Ridhai Chithaar II
>
> *While walking and sitting, sleeping and waking, contemplate within your heart the GurMantra.*
>
> (Guru Arjan Dev. Raag Maaroo 1006)

A key component to refining consciousness in Naam Symran is to listen to the recited sound; Whenever one's awareness drifts or is distracted by stimuli, such as, thought, sound, sensation, emotion, the practice is to become aware of its drift and then gently re-focus awareness on hearing the recitation of the Mantra. This helps the practitioner to internalize the meaning of the word and, more importantly, return one's attention to the word, enabling the cultivation of one-pointedness.

Suniai Laagai Sehaj Dhhiaan II
listening cultivates awareness intutively.
(Guru Nanak Dev Ji 4)

Saas Saas Prabh Manehi Samaalae II
Breath by breath bring Presence to your awareness.
(Raag Gauri: Guru Arjan Dev Ang 191 Line 7)

The three hall marks for meditation are:

- Stillness of body
- Silence of mind
- Spaciousness of awareness

Listening from a place of silence consciously helps and cultivates awareness. The combination of intention and attention become the hall mark of symran.

This on-going process increases awareness, which, consequently, leads to recognition of mental processes which gradually transforms the sense of self, and finally brings one to the door of ego-transcendence.

Listening ensures one does not simply slip into recitation of the mantra "parrot fashion", by consciously listening to the sound within it is possible to synchronise the mental recitation with the movement of the breath or "Sass Garass", gradually reducing the volume within until one rests in the silence. Stillness of body, silence of mind and spaciousness of awareness are the three markers of this practice.

Saahi Saahi Thujh Sanmalaa Kadhae N Visaaraeo II
With each and every breath, I dwell upon You; I shall never forget You.
(Sri Raag: Guru Nanak Dev 20)

Saas Giraas Japo Har Haree II4II29II42II
With every breath and morsel of food, I meditate on Har, Har."
(Guru Arjan Dev Ji 1148)

The names (mantras or shabds) of the Divine essence used in Naam-Symran fall into one of the following catergories

- Name of Essence
  Har – ha means "no sense of the body" – ra+i means "life given in you"
  Har, who is inhaling your breath
  WaheGuru – Wahe means wonderment, guru consists of two sounds, gu means formless, hidden and invisible power of Divinity
  ru means living beauty and luster in living beings.
- Qualitative names, Raam (immersed), Gobind (giver of universal energy,joy)
- Qualities of Transcendence and immanence: Akal (timeless), Wah (wonderment),
- Divine activities, Forgiver, sustainer,

ਆਪਣਾ ਆਪੁ ਪਛਾਣਿਆ ਨਾਮੁ ਨਿਧਾਨੁ ਪਾਇਆ ॥

Aapanaa Aap Pashhaaniaa naam Nidhhaan Paaeiaa ॥

One who realizes his own self, is blessed with the treasure of the naam.

(Raag Maaroo: Guru Nanak Dev Ang 1088)

Naam is the fruit of self-realisation; While shabd (sound) linked to Surat (attentive awareness) is the method of inner inquiry and introspection.

Life, Death and Rebirth

Why were you born? Gurmat addresses this central question;however, it is important to recognize that Gurmat does not accept the concept of an individualized single "soul" found in many other traditions. The embodied consciousness, or Atma is no different from the wave on an ocean, which may appear separate, but it is simply a manifesting component of the one ocean. As ultimate reality in nondual, there is only one non-dual Sat Chit and Anand, Existence-Consciousness-Joy, and cannot be divided. This reality, Brahman is described in terms that are spiritual yet utterly life and world affirming as Sat (i) the existence or substance that constitutes the universe (Existence), (ii) Chit - Consciousness that contains Existence, and (iii) Anand, non-dual blissfulness that expresses and experiences itself as Existence.

ਅਚਰਜ ਕਥਾ ਮਹਾ ਅਨੂਪ ॥
ਪ੍ਰਾਤਮਾ ਪਾਰਬ੍ਰਹਮ ਕਾ ਰੂਪ ॥ਰਹਾਉ॥

Acharaj Kaththaa Mehaa Anoop ll
Praathamaa Paarabreham Kaa Roop ll Rehaao ll
This descrilition is wonderous and incomparable
The very form of the Atma (individualised consciouness)
is Parbraham llPausell

(Raag Gond Guru Arjan Dev 868)

So what reincarnates? Every action has a reaction and appropriate consequences; Accordingly, one's birth is as a direct result of previous actions according to Gurmat. This determines your gender, race, place of birth, bound to specific parentage, individuals and life circumstances. Actions carried out as ego-complex bind the consequences of the actions to the ego-complex itself, which then determines the outcomes.

The actions committed as ego (sense of "I" the doer) during this present life determine the future lives, just as this moment of our mind, determines the next. When one dies, the energy connected with the ego-complex with all its pre-existing conditioning, preferences, abilities and characteristics that have been developed and conditioned in this life, re-establishes itself in a fertilized egg. Existence is pure consciousness, Parmatman/Universal Self (Ocean) and does not undergo birth and death. However, when embodied consciousness appears as a Jivaatama/individual self (wave) with imprints and impressions from previous ego based actions as the cause of "birth". Upon death, the body disintegrates however the jivaatama, (embodied consciousness) along with impressions created through ego-based actions, is reborn as another body, like a flame that appears continuous yet is distinct moment to moment.

This cycle, called Avaan-jaavan, coming and going, is a continuous cycle until the ego is transcended and duality is erased.

ਹਉਮੈ ਮੇਰਾ ਮਰੀ ਮਰੁ ਮਰਿ ਜੰਮੈ ਵਾਰੋ ਵਾਰ ॥

Houmai Maeraa Maree Mar Mar Janmai Vaaro Vaar II

Dying in egotism and self-conceit, one dies, and dies again, only to be reincarnated over and over again.
(Guru Nanak Dev Ang 1009)

ਹੰਉਮੈ ਅੰਦਰਿ ਖੜਕੁ ਹੈ ਖੜਕੇ ਖੜਕਿ ਵਿਹਾਇ ॥
ਹੰਉਮੈ ਵਡਾ ਰੋਗੁ ਹੈ ਮਰਿ ਜੰਮੈ ਆਵੈ ਜਾਇ ॥

Houmai Andhar Kharrak Hai Kharrakae Kharrak Vihaae II
Houmai Vaddaa Rog Hai Mar Janmai Aavai Jaae II

In egotism, one is assailed by fear; he passes his life totally troubled by fear.
Egotism is such a terrible disease; he dies, to be reincarnated - he continues coming and going.
(Raag Vadhans Guru Amar Das Ang:592)

Gurmat distinguishes how desires and anxieties experienced at the moment of death determine the next life. This process of dying and being reborn continues until the conditioning, craving and ignorance, cease. At the point when they cease, the mind attains the state of unconditioned mind, or Nirvanna.

ਜਿਤੁ ਲਾਗੋ ਮਨੁ ਬਾਸਨਾ ਅੰਤਿ ਸਾਈ ਪ੍ਰਗਟਾਨੀ ॥੬॥

Jith Laago Man Baasanaa Anth Saaee Pragattaanee II6II

That desire, to which the mind is attached, at the last moment, becomes manifest. II6II
(Raag Gauri Guru Arjan Dev Ang 242)

goojaree ||

a(n)th kaal jo lashhamee simarai aisee chi(n)thaa mehi jae marai ||

sarap jon val val aoutharai ||1||

aree baaee gobidh naam math beesarai || rehaao ||

a(n)th kaal jo eisathree simarai aisee chi(n)thaa mehi jae marai ||

baesavaa jon val val aoutharai ||2||

a(n)th kaal jo larrikae simarai aisee chi(n)thaa mehi jae marai ||

sookar jon val val aoutharai ||3||

a(n)th kaal jo ma(n)dhar simarai aisee chi(n)thaa mehi jae marai ||

praeth jon val val aoutharai ||4||

a(n)th kaal naaraaein simarai aisee chi(n)thaa mehi jae marai ||

badhath thilochan thae nar mukathaa peetha(n)bar vaa kae ridhai basai ||5||2||

Goojaree:

At the very last moment, one who thinks of wealth, and dies in such thoughts,

shall be reincarnated over and over again, in the form of serpents. ||1||

O sister, do not forget the naam. ||Pause||

At the very last moment, he who thinks of women, and dies in such thoughts,

shall be reincarnated over and over again as a prostitute. ||2||

At the very last moment, one who thinks of his children, and dies in such thoughts,

shall be reincarnated over and over again as a pig. ||3||

At the very last moment, one who thinks of mansions, and dies in such thoughts,

shall be reincarnated over and over again as a ghost. ||4||

At the very last moment, one who focuses on Narayana (name of Divine in all its infinite forms), and dies in such awareness, says Trilochan, that man shall be liberated; the Divine shall abide in his heart. ||5||2|

(Bhagat Trilochan Ji in Raag Gujri ang 526)

According to Gurmat, within the context of Oneness, unified non-dual existence, there is no death nor birth, and the apparent birth and death are the "illusionary" or transitory in which the forms change, relative to the unchanging consciousness. This understanding is conveyed in Gurmat in the following manner. While gold, copper and silver may look different, if these differences as taken as real, yet at the fundamental level of electrons, protons, neutrons or even further into the subatomic particles, ultimately, it's all energy and unified, albeit within its dualistic manifestation. Similarly, gold may appear to be one thing, but can be easily be transformed into a ring, a bangle, chain, or bracelet, gold can undergo transmigration or reincarnation as different forms.

ਜਨਮ ਮਰਨ ਕਾ ਭ੍ਰਮੁ ਗਇਆ ਗੋਬਿਦ ਲਿਵ ਲਾਗੀ ॥
ਜੀਵਤ ਸੁੰਨਿ ਸਮਾਨਿਆ ਗੁਰ ਸਾਖੀ ਜਾਗੀ ॥੧॥ਰਹਾਉ॥

Janam Maran Kaa Bhram Gaeiaa Gobidh Liv Laagee ||
Jeevath Sunn Samaaniaa Gur Saakhee Jaagee ||1|| Rehaaoll
The illusion of birth and death is gone; I lovingly focus on the Lord of the Universe.
In my life, I am absorbed in deep silent meditation; the Guru's Teachings have awakened me. ||1||Pause||
(Raag Bilaaval Bhagat Kabir Ang:857)

Accepting death and relinquishing clinging to self preservation

Gurmat lays great emphasis on being mindful of ones' certain mortality, and its acceptance. Birth as creation and death as dissolution are a continuous process in every aspect of life, to be Present is the awareness of this process in the present moment itself. This provides a fundamental key to cultivating a balanced and healing life style, learning to accept change and let-go or the constant grasping for "happiness" or permanency.

Awareness of one own mortality shifts individual's intrinsic goals, engendering humility, change of priorities, enriching the experience of life in the present moment.

Acceptance of own death instigates intimacy in relationships while also initiates an innate sense of gratitude, acceptance and openness or optimism. Symran (skt. Smrti or mindfulness) is also translated as sym (mindful) + maran (death), mindfulness of death.

Clinging to life and unaware of ones' own death, create a false sense of permanency. This is further reinforced by clinging to goals and objects of cravings, which in turn keep awareness fused with "future output" and become essential to ones' happiness or fulfilment (satisfaction). This identification with the belief that the goals or objects of desires would provide the illusionary happiness promised by every consumer product maintains awareness future oriented and misses out on the experience of here and now.

Future oriented thinking is accompanied by anxiety, worry and frustration, all of which impact the body's' physiology and over time create a toxic internal environment within.

ਪਹਿਲਾ ਮਰਣੁ ਕਬੂਲਿ ਜੀਵਣ ਕੀ ਛਡਿ ਆਸ ॥

Pehilaa Maran Kabool Jeevan Kee Shhadd Aas II

First, accept death, and give up any hope of life.

(Raag Maaroo Guru Arjan Dev Ang:1102)

Anxieties and fear generated by this encounter with mortality is addressed internally through meditation on Naam (Naam Symran or mindfulness on Naam) and externally through engaging in ethical selfless service (seva) towards existence. (sggs 176).

ਜਨਮੁ ਜੀਤਿ ਮਰਣਿ ਮਨੁ ਮਾਨਿਆ ॥
ਆਪਿ ਮੂਆ ਮਨੁ ਮਨ ਤੇ ਜਾਨਿਆ ॥
ਨਜਰਿ ਭਈ ਘਰੁ ਘਰ ਤੇ ਜਾਨਿਆ ॥੨॥

Janam Jeeth Maran Man Maaniaa II
Aap Mooaa Man Man Thae Jaaniaa II
Najar Bhee Ghar Ghar Thae Jaaniaa II2II

*So win the game of life; let your mind surrender and accept
death.*

*When the self dies, the individual mind comes to know the
Supreme Mind.*

*As the inner vision is awakened, one comes to know one's
own home, deep within the self.*

(Raag Gauri Guru Nanak Dev Ang:153)

Jeevan Mukti – self-actualization, self-realisation and self-sovereignty

Jeevan Mukti refers to living beyond ego-transcendence; a life which begins in duality, "I" and "I" (Existence) including Presence in the heart, through the practice of Naam Symran and grace, one develops towards transcendence of individuality which manifests in a variety of experiences, forms of Unity and ultimately into a self(lessness)-realized life, having transcended the ego-complex into non-dual pure consciousness. This overcomes self-imposed limitations of the conditioned mind and freedom from the bondage of the ego-body complex, haumai.

Jeevan mukti is achieved through Naam Symran, a contemplative practice known as prayer of the heart, Hesychasm, Dhirk, atam-gyan or atam-veechar. This method of mindfulness consists of the uninterrupted repetition of a specific mantra paced with the breath and accompanied by focusing attention on the sense of self in a specific part of the chest known as the Hirdya or heart. The practice of Naam Symran inevitably lead the practitioner into direct intuition or sehaj avasta, which enables one to "see" God, followed by ontopoiesis, recognizing the ordering in the unfolding of existence, finally ending as an experience of pure consciousness, a non-dual, unifiedconsciousness experience as one wholeness.

The ego-transcendence process can be considered to take place in several stages which include

1. Jaap – Procession of Naam-symran practice from verbal to internal breath paced repetition of a mantra and listening to the sound
2. Focus on the internalization towards the chest (Hirdya)
3. Ajaap jaap – Replacement from intentional repetition of mantra with spontaneous emergence from within
4. Viraag – Detachment
5. Ardas – dissolution of repetition towards a wordless sustained presence, spontaneous innovation for mergence
6. Anand – a state of complete, self-surrender in an experience of ever-present Presence which finally leads to "Anand" or non-dual Oneness.

ਕਿਉ ਕਰਿ ਇਹੁ ਮਨੁ ਮਾਰੀਐ ਕਿਉ ਕਰਿ ਮਿਰਤਕੁ ਹੋਇ ॥
ਕਹਿਆ ਸਬਦੁ ਨ ਮਾਨਈ ਹਉਮੈ ਛਡੈ ਨ ਕੋਇ ॥
ਗੁਰ ਪਰਸਾਦੀ ਹਉਮੈ ਛੁਟੈ ਜੀਵਨ ਮੁਕਤੁ ਸੋ ਹੋਇ ॥
ਨਾਨਕ ਜਿਸ ਨੋ ਬਖਸੇ ਤਿਸੁ ਮਿਲੈ ਤਿਸੁ ਬਿਘਨੁ ਨ ਲਾਗੈ ਕੋਇ ॥੨॥

Kio Kar Eihu Man Maareeai Kio Kar Mirathak Hoe II
Kehiaa Sabadh N Maanee Houmai Shhaddai N Koe II
Gur Parasaadhee Houmai Shhuttai Jeevan Mukath So
   Hoe II
Naanak Jis No Bakhasae This Milai This Bighan N Laagai
   Koe II2II

How can this mind be conquered? How can it be killed?
If one does not accept the Word of the Shabad, egotism
   does not depart.
By Guru's Grace, egotism is eradicated, and then, one is
   Jivan Mukta - liberated while yet alive.
O Nanak, one whom is forgiven is united, and then no
   obstacles block the way. II2II

(Ang:948)

Gurmat provides a detailed insight into the process of ego-transcendence which help break down the psychological changes, character changes, inner transformation which includes a personal psycho-spiritual ethical stand point and self-sovereignty. The absence of one's sense of separate-self or Haumai enables the individuals to transcend duality and change the way to relating to events, including pain and pleasure, experiencing both as transient

> prabh kee aagiaa aatham hithaavai ||
> jeevan mukath sooo kehaavai ||
> thaisaa harakh thaisaa ous sog ||
> sadhaa ana(n)dh theh nehee bioug ||
> thaisaa suvaran thaisee ous maattee ||
> thaisaa a(n)mrith thaisee bikh khaattee ||
> thaisaa maan thaisaa abhimaan ||
> thaisaa ra(n)k thaisaa raajaan ||
> jo varathaaeae saaee jugath ||
> naanak ouhu purakh keheeai jeevan mukath ||7||
>
> *One who, in their individualised consciousness, accepts*
>   *Will of God, (acceptance of Hukam),*
> *is said to be Jivan Mukta - liberated while yet alive.*
> *As is joy, so is sorrow to him.*
> *He is in eternal bliss, and is not separated from God.*
> *As is gold, so is dust to him.*
> *As is ambrosial nectar, so is bitter poison to him.*
> *As is honour, so is dishonour.*
> *As is the beggar, so is the king.*
> *Whatever unfolds, that is his way.*
> *O Nanak, that being is known as Jivan Mukta. ||7||*

ਜੀਵਨ ਮੁਕਤ ਜਗਦੀਸ ਜਪਿ ਮਨ ਧਾਰਿ ਰਿਦ ਪਰਤੀਤਿ ॥

Jeevan Mukath Jagadhees Jap Man Dhhaar Ridh
   Paratheeth ||

Become Jivan-mukta, liberated while yet alive, by meditating
   on the Source of the Universe, O mind, and maintaining
   faith in Him in your heart.

                    (Raag Goojree: Guru Arjan Dev Ang 508 Line 11)

ਜਿਸੁ ਨਾਮੁ ਰਿਦੈ ਸੋ ਜੀਵਨ ਮੁਕਤਾ ॥

Jis Naam Ridhai So Jeevan Mukathaa II

One who keeps the Naam in his heart is Jivan-mukta, liberated while yet alive.

(Raag Bhaira-o: Guru Arjan Dev Ang 1156 Line 1)

Gurmukh – Self-actualised, self-realised and self-sovereign

Self-actualisation was first brought to the Western psychological worldview by Abraham Maslow (1954); He researched healthy individuals as opposed to sick ones. Through his research of healthy individuals, he proposed that every human being has a natural drive to healthiness, or self-actualization. Once the basic, biological,safety and psychological needs have been fulfilled, it enables the desire for the higher levels of realization. He also considered that we have the natural, unconscious and innate capacity to seek own needs and shine through. (Maslow 1968)

Maslow "Self- actualization means experiencing fully, vividly, selflessly, with full concentration and total absorption" (The Farther Reaches of Human Nature, p. 45). Self-actualisation therefore represents the optimal psychological condition for all humans. The process of self-actualisation leads to optimum mental health and well-being; a self-actualised individual is on the path towards becoming a Gurmukh.

ਬਿਨੁ ਗੁਰ ਪ੍ਰੀਤਿ ਨ ਉਪਜੈ ਹਉਮੈ ਮੈਲੁ ਨ ਜਾਇ ॥
ਸੋਹੰ ਆਪੁ ਪਛਾਣੀਐ ਸਬਦਿ ਭੇਦਿ ਪਤੀਆਇ ॥
ਗੁਰਮੁਖਿ ਆਪੁ ਪਛਾਣੀਐ ਅਵਰ ਕਿ ਕਰੇ ਕਰਾਇ ॥੯॥

Bin Gur Preeth N Oopajai Houmai Mail N Jaae II
Sohan Aap Pashhaaneeai Sabadh Bhaedh Patheeaae II
Guramukh Aap Pashhaaneeai Avar K Karae Karaae II9II

Without the Guru, love does not well up, and the filth of egotism does not depart.

*One who recognizes within himself that, "He is me", and
who is pierced through by the Shabad, is satisfied.
When one becomes Gurmukh and realizes his own self,
what more is there left to do or have done? ||9||*

(Sri Raag Guru Nanak Dev)

Gurmat defines the process of self-actualsiation, self-realisation towards self-soverignity per the stages below. "Artha" represents the basic physical and security needs of a human being, which once met, highlight the next set of needs, and those are associated with emotional fulfilment. This according to Gurmat comes from "Gristi jeevan" (life of a householder) engaged with relationships, partnerships, family, social and environment.

ਸੋ ਗਿਰਹੀ ਸੋ ਦਾਸੁ ਉਦਾਸੀ ਜਿਨਿ ਗੁਰਮੁਖਿ ਆਪੁ ਪਛਾਨਿਆ ॥
ਨਾਨਕੁ ਕਹੈ ਅਵਰੁ ਨਹੀ ਦੂਜਾ ਸਾਚ ਸਬਦਿ ਮਨੁ ਮਾਨਿਆ ॥੫॥੧੭॥

So Girehee So Dhaas Oudhaasee Jin Guramukh Aap
Pashhaaniaa ||
Naanak Kehai Avar Nehee Dhoojaa Saach Sabadh Man
Maaniaa ||5||17||

*He is a householder, he is a renunciate and God's slave,
who, as Gurmukh, realizes his own self.
Says Nanak, his mind is pleased and appeased by the True
Word of the Shabad; there is no other at all. ||5||17||*

(Raag Parbhati Guru Nanak Dev SGGS 1332)

Meeting emotional needs gives rise to ethical needs. Something that is currently being witnessed in developed countries as the "Green movement" or eco-friendly and environmentally aware moments. However, the foundation of this ethical development is manifold. It begins with the cultivation of contentment and present moment awareness. This practice matures into self-compassion and compassion. It is from this fertile personal subjective experience, that personal ethics begin to emerge, founded on "do no harm", including to one self. Present moment awareness over time enables the recognition of Hukam, or the unfolding of the present moment by moment experience, existence, and impermanence. The recognisition of Hukam is indictive of Vivek Buddhi, matured discerning intellect. This discerning intellect matures with compassion and develops positive psychological states of gratitude, optimism, joyfulness, all of which are recognised as grace. The recognition of impermanence inevitably leads towards detachment and dispassion.

The second part of ethical development provides an indepth experientially verified understanding of the Guru, emobodied consciousness and Consciouness as the ground of all existence. The whole process has a profound transformational impact the ego-bound individuals, modifying character, traits, cultivating positive psychological states and in cultivating a deep sense of unity. The characterists of self-actualisation in table below.

Jeevan Mukti Self-Soverignity

Mokhsa Release

Dharma – Ethical Needs Atma, Paratma, Guru

Dharma – Ethical Needs Symran, Hukam, Vivek, Nardir, Virag

Kama/Emotional needs Gristi/Sangat Kudrat, humanity, family, relationships

Artha/Physical needs – Kirpan Security, protection, law, limits, frameworks

Artha/Physical needs – Langar Basic life needs, air, water, food, shelter, warmth, sleep

Taoist	Zen Buddhist	Maslow	Sikhi (Gurmat)
Sage	State of perfection	Self actualised	Self actualised
• Openness to life	• Non-attachment	• Optimum psychological condition	• Sahej – inner harmony
• Tranquillity	• Absence to rigidity	• Accurate perception of reality	• Self-aware
• Simplicity	• Inner harmony	• High level of creativity	• Accurate perception of reality
• Authenticity	• State of perfection	• Few defences	• Authentic
• Compassionate	• No division between thought and action	• Integrated	• Ethical
• Transcend duality	• Absence of rigidity	• Personal autonomy	• Compassionate
• Indifference to worldly affairs while involved in them	• Non-attachment to thing	• Unconventional ethics	• Autonomous
• Receptivity	• Free to make choice	• Human kinship	• Tranquil
• Contentment	• Personal autonomy	• Compassionate	• Simple lifestyle
• Intellectual honesty	• receptive	• Humble	• Contentment
• Unassuming attitude	• Content	• Deep interpersonal relationship	• Honest
• Sense of responsibility	• Intellectually honest	• Respect for others	• Modest
• Determination	• Free to make choice	• Ongoing personal growth	• Unassuming
	• Personal autonomy	• Detached	• Humble
	• Sense of responsibility	• Openness to nature and others	• Receptive
	• Personal authority	• Self-regard	• Responsible
	• Transcendence from birth and death	• Inner freedom	• Detached
		• Yearning spiritual life	• Desirelessness
		• Non-materialistic	• Self-disciplined
		• Scepticism of science	• Selflessness
			• Spontaneous

Below is a table which compares the characteristic of self-actualised individual from the work of Maslow, Taoism, Zen Buddhism and Sikhi traditions.

Gurmat identifies evolutionary states and stages of consciousness as part of the transpersonal process and ego transcendence because of contemplative practices of symran and naam symran or prayer of the heart. These psychospiritual states are referred to as Bhagat, Sant, Gyani, Bharmgyani, Khalsa, Satguru, and Mahapurekh The Sikh sacred scriptures, the Sri Guru Granth Sahib provides a detailed and sophisticated understanding of these altered states of consciousness which have not been included in this publication.

Pavan Guru and Shabad Guru, Breath and Sound

In Gurmat the breath and the shabad (specific mantras) are considered as the Guru (authentic teachers), and the body is never a Guru; Shabad has always been the Guru and it resides in everyone and gives light to all creation. Through the practice of Naam Symran – sound seeded meditation, combining intention, attention and vibrational energy, allow awareness to become aware of itself. Awareness can only be known by becoming aware. This is Gurmat marag (the Gurmat path) and indicates to a Sikh – (student of life) the destination.

ਪਵਣੁ ਗੁਰੁ ਪਾਣੀ ਪਿਤਾ ਮਾਤਾ ਧਰਤਿ ਮਹਤੁ ॥

Pavan guroo Paanee Pithaa Maathaa Dhharath Mehath ॥

Air is the guru, Water is the Father, and Earth is the Great Mother of all.

(Salok: Guru Nanak Dev Ang 8)

In the context of Gurmat psycho-spiritual approach, breath and sound, both separately and combined offer a powerful and effective method to cultivate psycho-spiritual health and facilitate one's progress towards ego-transcendence and unification.Both the breath and Shabad enable consciousness to open to one's innate wisdom, which,through sustained practice, expand awareness and depth of life experience. The breath is sacred, an anchor and a teacher which introduces one to the path of inner discovery, mental health, Present moment, Presence, impermanence and life itself.

As functioning biological organisms, our functions are regulated and influenced through our sensory and nervous systems. Our internal organs function is influenced by the autonomic nervous system (ANS), which is a division of the peripheral nervous system. The autonomic nervous system is a control system that acts largely unconsciously and regulates bodily functions such as the heart rate, digestion, respiratory rate, pupillary response, urination, and sexual arousal.

This system is the primary mechanism in control of the fight-or-flight response and the freeze-and-dissociate response.[17]

The ANS has two branches, one which is considered as a flight-fight response system, the sympathetic nervous system and the other, parasympathetic nervous system as the "rest and digest" or "feed and breed" system. Both systems work in relation to one another, and have "opposite" actions where one system activates a physiological response and the other inhibits it.[18]

Breath is the bridge between the voluntary and autonomic nervous system, while we do not require conscious attention to breathe, bringing attention to the breath immediately activates the healing and nurturing potential of the breath.[19]

Non-judgemental focus on the breath has the capacity

to heal and re-balance us because much of our emotional and psychological suffering arises from "automatic" unconscious reactions and routines. For example, when people feel anxious they resort to smoking, or turn to alcohol to numb unpleasant emotions or lash out "automatically" when feeling angry or threatened.Conscious awareness of our breath enables us to **"take control"**, to become mindful or aware of patterns of reaction and therefore choose our response rather than react

Non-judgemental, intentional focus on the breath helps to cultivate mental peace and tranquillity. Combining breath and mantra, accompanied with focusing attention on the sense of self in the chest facilitates the transcendence of the sense of separate ego, followed by state of unification or oneness.

Sound or vibration as the mantra is the teacher or Guru, while our focused attention listening to the sound of the mantra internally becomes the disciple. Through this practise one can go beyond sensations, emotions, thoughts towards silence, emptiness and Presence.

ਸਬਦੁ ਗੁਰੂ ਸੁਰਤਿ ਧੁਨਿ ਚੇਲਾ ॥

Sabadh Guroo Surath Dhhun Chaelaa ||

Shabad is the guru, awareness is the disciple.

(Raag Raamkali: Guru Nanak Dev Ang 943)

This inner journey of listening to the mantra being recited enables awareness to follow the sound into increasingly deeper states of consciousness. Speech has four forms, provided here in reverse order. Utterance with the aid of the tongue and mouth is known as "Viakhari", before which comes "Madham", communication to the tongue, which is preceded by "Pasanti", suggestion to the mind, which begins from "Para" and has its origin in the abstract mind. Through dedicated practice of Naam-Symran awareness is drawn from "Viakhari" until it arrives in "Para" or beyond.

The breath itself is a constant Mantra from one's conception to one's death. The physical manifestation of breathing contains within the inhalation and exhalation two distinct sounds, "So," on the breath in and "Ha", pronounced "hum," on the breath out. In this practice, "So-ham" is the mantra which is heard during the movement of the breath; once again the practice requires a relaxed state with alert awareness focused on the Ajaapa-jaap mantra heard.

> Nanak sohan hamsa japu japahu
> Tribhavan tasai samahi.
> *He is me and I am he*
> *The three worlds are included in the One.*
>
> (Guru Nanak Dev Ji)

CHAPTER TWO

Mental Health and Well Being

Mental Health – Klesha

Psychology is about human mental health and wellbeing, however, current post-colonial definitions of mental health are far from adequate and do not reflect mental health beyond the ego and completely dismiss the importance of spirituality within health and wellbeing. The definition of mental health in Western psychology has a broad spectrum which defines mental health against criteria drawn up according to the Diagnostic and Statistical Manual of Mental disorders. (DSM IV).

The Diagnostic and Statistical Manual (*DSM*) of the American Psychiatric Association, was developed in 1952 post world war II as a way of categorizing mental illness and is considered *the* reference for the characterization and diagnosis of mental disorders. It is important to recognize that the DSM characterization of mental illness is not based on science but on the majority consensus from psychologists and psychiatrists.[20]

While the objective of the DSM as with all its previous editions, is to provide a common language for describing psychopathology. The DSM characterization of mental illness may provide the same language, but it fundamentally lacks validity, which unlike definitions of diabetes, CVD, ischemic heart disease, or AIDS, the DSM diagnoses are based on a consensus about clusters of clinical symptoms, not any objective laboratory measure.

They range from feelings of loneliness right through to severe schizophrenia. Western psychology defines mental illness as the psychological and behavioral patterns that are different from the "norm", including comprehending reality in terms of impermanence, mind-body connection and interconnection.

The question invariably arises, since Western psychology is less than 150 years old, and in its embryonic stage about understanding the nature of mind and has failed to recognize and include Consciousness within its mental model, how can it define mental illness when it does not understand the nature of the mind, let alone go beyond the mind?

Western psychological understanding of mind and mental health is incomplete, it can be better defined as ego-fixing, within its definitions of healthy ego-complex and unhealthy ego-complex. Treatment of mental health according to western psychology is more about developing a "healthier" and "normalized" ego than recognizing the root causes of mental illness, which invariably is the mind as "Haumai" or ego-complex.

Gurmat provides a definition of mental illness from a psycho-spiritual and psycho-physiological stand point, and defines the root of mental illness as identity fused with a conceptualized self, or haumai (ego-complex), termed manmukh. Manmukh is being ignorant about ones' mind and being fused or identified with the mind and its content without any awareness of "having a mind" but not being the mind. By identifying with the mental construct as self inevitably disconnect one from consciousness itself.

The mind can be easily conditioned through education,

authority and social interaction, an identity fused with the content of the mind enslaves the individuals within its own mental prison consisting of manufactured worldview, ingrained beliefs, concepts and opinions. In addition, the manmukh can be easily manipulated into behavior which is both destructive to oneself, but also humanity, environment and society.

The impact of manipulating conditioned minds is evident across society and covers a range of behavior from compulsive consumerism, activated through endless advertising for products to make one feel "complete", "happy", and "self-worth", right through to murder, massacre and torture to "protect the faith", "bringing democracy" or the famous "weapons of mass destruction" used to destroy and bring carnage across the world.[21] Defining depression, anxiety, fear, panic attacks as mental illness deals with the symptoms of mental illness and not its root cause, as there is minimal understanding of anything beyond the ego-complex. Additionally, definition of mental illness is culturally bound, and since the Anglo-American empire is the dominant and aggressive colonizing culture with its own homogenous worldview, both mental health and mental illness are being defined according to this limited, distorted and destructive worldview.

Indic thought defined the main characteristics of mental illness as the manifestation of "Klesha" or mental pollution or distress. The cause of klesha can be traced back to ignorance (avidya or agyan) and trisanaa (craving) of the Haumai (ego-complex) towards pleasure and away from suffering or perceived suffering. The arising of unhealthy mental states is termed klesha, these are psychological and emotional states that are harmful and unwholesome, and impact our physiology, behavior, produce painful results, worsen our physical health, and distort our priorities and sense of wellbeing.[22]

ਹਉਮੈ ਰੋਗੁ ਵਡਾ ਸੰਸਾਰਿ ॥

Haumai Rog Vaddaa Sansaar ||

The world is suffering from the terrible disease of egotism.
(Raag Malar: Guru Amar Das Ang 1278)

Mental illness or Klesha results from fusion with our ego-complex

Mental illnessor Klesha is conditioned reactions of our ego complex

Gurmat defines five primary harmful psychological states

Mental illness or Klesha arises because of ego-complex reaction to stimuli

Mental illness or klesha distort perceptions

Mental illness or Klesha is impermanent as its conditioned reactions

Mental states or Klesha directly impact physiology (mind-body connection)

Mental health or Klesha can be resolved through right-mindfulness and Naam Symran (mindfulness with somatic focus designed for ego-transcendence)

Klesha – destructive and harmful psychological states

Klesha is etymologically derived from the root meaning "to adhere, to stick or stickiness", the root of mental and emotional suffering. Klesha is an effect of the conditioned mind, (haumai) that gives rise to suffering, affliction, pain and conflict and is an inherent quality of the human experience. In terms of psychology, klesha represent the foundational catalyst for mental illness and psychological distress.[23]

There are five primary klesha that distort perceptions and influence both physiological reactions and behavior. These five klesha give rise to psychological suffering and bind the ego-complex together with the embodied consciousness (jeev atma) into a cycle of repetition, both in terms of psychological states as well as birth, death and reincarnation.

1. Avidya, Ignorance and misapprehension about reality
2. Asmitâ, Haumai or the erroneous identification of the Self with the conditioned ego-complex.
3. Raga, attraction
4. Dvesa, aversion
5. Abhinivesham self-preservation mode, fearing elimination and clinging to life

The primary klesha is the inability to know ones' own mind or the nature of ones' mind. Due to not knowing the mind, let alone its nature, one creates mental constructs about subject and objects and clings to them as real. Attachment and aversion are the result of ignorance, attachment to objects, people, beliefs that make one happy and aversion against objects, people, beliefs and so on that make one unhappy.

Avidya (ignorance) is *the basis of suffering. It is ignorance of the nature of reality*, misconception of the true nature of reality, including ourselves, believing the temporary and impermanent nature of Existence to be eternal and that *'I am my body, emotions, mind, and intellect:* Not knowing ones' own mind or its nature is called "Avidya" and mistakenly fused with the content of the mind, yet ignorant of the clear and emptiness of consciousness. This lack of understanding about reality and self is the root klesha and produces the other Kleshas.

Asmita (I-am-ness or I-am-maker) is the false identification with the body, including the content of our mind and emotions. Haumai then becomes our conditioned sense of self, trapping us both externally and internally.

Raga (attachment) is the attachment to thoughts, beliefs, feelings, body and things that reinforce the sense of self or "me" and provide a sense of permanency to the ego-complex. The cravings for experiences of pleasure and permanency distort priorities and trigger mindless actions and myopic vision. When one fails to obtain the object of desire, it triggers unpleasant emotions, and suffering. On the other hand, when the objects of desires are obtained, the accompanying pleasant experiences quickly fade away and trap the ego-complex in an endless cycle of cravings to repeat the experience or maintain it.

Dvesha (aversion or repulsion) is the opposite of raga, and the other side of the same coin as Raga or attachment. It is the repulsion or avoidance of unpleasant or uncomfortable experiences. This mental state of non-acceptance of one type of experience, and craving of another less-uncomfortable experience perpetuates both psychological and physiological suffering and traps the ego-complex is a constant state of psychological discomfort or mentally unhealthy states. The avoidance of "what is" or non-acceptance of the experience itself creates discomfort and detrimentally changes the body's' physiology over a period.

Abhinivesham is the avoidance of death and continuous clinging to life. Self-preservation is the amongst the deepest of klesha and gives rise to many types of suffering especially within modern educated societies, which have trapped people in the unfruitful search of permanent life, eternal youth and anti-ageing to the point that it's become an acceptable form of self-harm through cosmetic surgery and other types of procedures to remain youthful.

ਹਉਮੈ ਰੋਗਿ ਜਾ ਕਾ ਮਨੁ ਬਿਆਪਿਤ ਓਹੁ ਜਨਮਿ ਮਰੈ ਬਿਲਲਾਤੀ ॥੨॥

Haumai Rog Jaa Kaa Man Biaapith Ouhu Janam Marai Bilalaathee ||2||

One whose mind is afflicted by the disease of egotism,
cries out in birth and death.

(Raag Sorath: Guru Arjan Dev Ang 610 Line 4)

ਹਉਮੈ ਮੇਰਾ ਵਡ ਰੋਗੁ ਹੈ ਵਿਚਹੁ ਠਾਕਿ ਰਹਾਇ ॥੨੧॥

Haumai Maeraa Vadd Rog Hai Vichahu Thaak Rehaae ||21||

Egotism and self-conceit are terrible diseases; tranquility
and stillness come from within.

(Raag Suhi: Guru Amar Das. Ang 756)

ਦੂਜੈ ਭਾਇ ਅਗਿਆਨੁ ਦੁਹੇਲਾ ॥੪॥

Dhoojai Bhaae Agiaan Dhuhaelaa ||4||

In the love of duality and ignorance, you shall suffer.

(Raag Gauri: Guru Nanak Dev Ang 226)

ਮਿਥਿਆ ਸੰਗਿ ਸੰਗਿ ਲਪਟਾਏ ਮੋਹ ਮਾਇਆ ਕਰਿ ਬਾਧੇ ॥

Mithhiaa Sang Sang Lapattaaeae Moh Maaeiaa Kar Baadhhae ||

They are attached to falsehood; clinging to the transitory,
they are trapped in emotional attachment to Maya.

(Raag Asa: Guru Arjan Dev Ang 402)

ਲਪਟਿ ਰਹਿਓ ਰਸਿ ਲੋਭੀ ਪਤੰਗ ॥

Lapatt Rehiou Ras Lobhee Pathang ||

You cling to worldly pleasures like a greedy moth.

(Raag Gauri Sukhmanee: Guru Arjan Dev Ang 283)

While klesha are fundamental to human experience and cause of suffering, Gurmat provides the solution to transforming harmful psychological states into healthier and wholesome states through the practice of Symran, Naam Symran and selfless service.

ਮਨ ਮਹਿ ਲਾਗੈ ਸਾਚੁ ਧਿਆਨੁ ॥
ਮਿਟਹਿ ਕਲੇਸ ਸੁਖੀ ਹੋਇ ਰਹੀਐ ॥

Man Mehi Laagai Saach Dhhiaan ||
Mittehi Kalaes Sukhee Hoe Reheeai ||

*With the mind centered in meditation on Presence,
(unchanging present moment)
Anguish is eradicated, and one comes to dwell in peace.*
(Raag Gauri Guaarayree Guru Arjan Dev Ang:183)

ਜਿਸੁ ਗੁਰ ਪ੍ਰਸਾਦਿ ਤੂਟੈ ਹਉ ਰੋਗੁ ॥
ਨਾਨਕ ਸੋ ਜਨੁ ਸਦਾ ਅਰੋਗੁ ॥

Jis Gur Prasaadh Thoottai Ho Rog ll
Naanak So Jan Sadhaa Arog ll2ll
*One who, by Guru's Grace, is cured of the disease of ego
Nanak, that person is forever healthy. ll2ll*
(Raag Gauri Sukhmanee Guru Arjan Dev Ang:282)

Psychophysiology is the relationship between Haumai (psychological sense of self, or "me") and its impact on the body's physiology. The root cause of disease is Raga and Dvesha, the tendencies for our ego-complex to crave pleasure and avoid non-pleasure and suffering.

Raga and Dvesha constitute our experience of the world of phenomena. Raga-Dvesha is a result of our illusionary sense of self, (hau) and its reaction to experiences results in likes and dislikes, that trigger our threat or motivation response cycles, which in turn impact our biochemistry and physiology creating a toxic internal environment that gives rise to cause for diseases (Adhi and Vyadhi).

Raga and Dvesha are the root of disease as they impact the body's physiology, altering the body's homeostatic balance, changing blood pressure, hormonal levels in addition to a host of other biochemical changes that give rise to internal conditions which lead to cellular malfunction, inflammation and consequently illness and disease.

Haumai, is our psychological sense of self, identified with the body, beliefs, options, emotions and desires. The instinctive response of our Haumai to real or perceived threats and danger trigger our self-preservation process, including the threat-stress-response, flight, fight or freeze system, which is experienced both psychologically and physiologically.

During these periods of threats, physiological changes include release of glucose, cortisol, lipids, adrenaline, and reduction in blood vessel diameter, increased blood pressure, and diversions of blood away from the stomach into the muscles. Prolonged periods of internal physiological conditions create a toxic environment in which disease and cell malfunction begin to manifest, leading to physical illnesses. Our physiology behaves in the same way when we experience stress, anger, physical, emotional or psychological demands.

While the response to threats is an evolutionary and necessary mechanism, ongoing psychological threats create mental and emotional states in which flight becomes self-isolation, fight become self-criticism and freeze becomes self-absorption or getting absorbed in our thoughts which in turn perpetuate the threat-stress-response, generating yet more negative emotions and worsening the physiological impact and general health. This flight-fight-freeze mechanism contributes towards depression, stress, anxiety, anger and loneliness. In other words, a range of mental illnesses can be seen to have their roots in being trapped in this cycle.

Gurmat identifies five psychological states which are responsible for triggering physiological reactions and thus, if uncontrolled, will inevitably lead to toxic physiological conditions including increased production of glucose, cortisol, epinephrine changes in blood pressure, heart rate and renal function. This creates a highly toxic environment within the body, which increases blood acidity, blood coagulation agents and changes gene activity of immune cells before they enter the bloodstream so that they are ready to fight infection or trauma which then lead to inflammation.[24]

		Activity	Impact of bio systems
Kaam	Sensual craving	Seeking sensual gratification	Activate excitement response system
Krodh	Anger	Avoiding suffering	Activate threat response system
Lobh	Greed or craving	Seeking pleasure	Activate excitement &/or threat response systems
Moh	Emotional attachment	Seeking permanency through attachments	Activate threat &/or excitement response system
Ahamkaar	I-am-maker	Seeking Self assertion	Cause for grasping and attachments when ever these two activities are threatened or give rise to anger.

These five states directly influence our autonomic nervous system (ANS), triggering the flight-fight response system, which in turn impacts heart rate, digestion, breathing, blood pressure and arousal.[25,26]

Kaam, karodh, lobh, moh and ahamkara are referred as the "five thieves". These emotional states tend to hijack awareness by fusing it with the content of the mind and drive the thinking process. These emotional states are self-perpetuating, diverting awareness from the present, embedding it either in the future or the past.

Emotions such as anger, greed driven excitement, sexual arousal and attachment are all linked to increased autonomic nervous system (ANS) and reduced para sympathetic activity.

Increase activity of the autonomic nervous system (ANS) results in physiological and biological changes within the body. These changes include increase in cortisol, adrenaline, higher blood pressure, blood glucose level changes, to mention but a few. These changes if maintained damage the cellular function. Cells respond to changes activated by the ANS activity in various ways ranging from the activation of survival pathways to the initiation of cell death that eventually eliminates damaged cells. Depending on the type of cell, and the duration of changes activated by the ANS activity determine whether the cells will respond to protect or destroy themselves.[25,26]

Emotions operate as feedback mechanisms to our motives. We experience unpleasant emotional states when our awareness is focused on threats to our self or those we care about, they may be real or imagined threats. Pleasant emotions are experienced as achievement, contentment and joy, when we feel safe, secure and present.

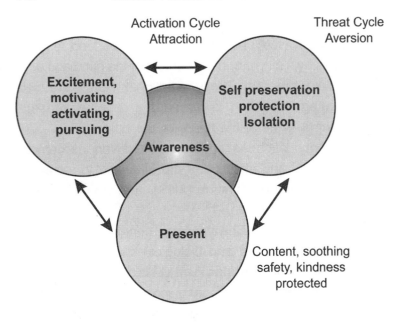

Hukam, acceptance and psychological suffering

ਹੁਕਮੈ ਬੁਝੈ ਨਿਰਾਸਾ ਹੋਈ ॥

Hukamai Boojhai Niraasaa Hoee ||

Understanding Hukam makes one desire less.

(Raag Asa: Guru Amar Das Ang 423)

Suffering (Dukh) can be defined as psycho-emotional states experienced as anxiety, stress, panic, depression and so on which are experienced subjectively as discomfort or unpleasant experiences. These experiences result from the interaction between our perceived sense of reality and reality as it is. Our sense organs (gyan Indira) are the gateways of stimuli to our mind, which catalase the reaction or responses from our, Haumai, or sense of separate self.

This does not mean that these emotional states are "bad" or others are "good", emotional states are feedback mechanism, interpreted through our senses, judgement, intellect and attention, they form our interaction with the world.

Acceptance is related to the ego-complex and is a fundamental component for the development of mental health and well-being. Acceptance does not mean resignation, nor does it mean that one must like one's experience. Acceptance is acknowledgmentof the experience for what It feels like without running away from it, contracting from it or distracting from it. Acceptance is the cultivation of a non-judgmental attitude. Acceptance is non-resistance, defined as "living within the Hukam" in Gurmat.

Non-acceptance or resistance is the catalyst for many form of mental illness, including anxiety, depression, fear and anger based responses, especially when the non-acceptance is focused on self-image, self-worth, unpleasant feelings, thoughts or sensations.

Acceptance is learning to first allow and be open to the experience before responding to change it towards a more palatable experience. Acceptance requires the cultivation of awareness, kindness to oneself and commitment.

Recognition and realizing the play of the ever Present Hukam provides one with the mental scaffolding for the development of alternative strategies to resistance and non-acceptance, and helps in the formation of a healthy non-judgmental attitude which empower us to transform both our internal environment and that which requires change

ਇਕਸ ਸਿਉ ਮਨੁ ਮਾਨਿਆ ਤਾ ਹੋਆ ਨਿਹਚਲੁ ਚੀਤੁ ॥

Eikas Sio Man Maaniaa Thaa Hoaa Nihachal Cheeth ||

When the mind accepts, and is satisfied with the One, then the consciousness becomes steady and stable.

(Sri Raag: Guru Arjan Dev Ang 44)

ਜੋ ਤੁਮ੍ ਕਰਹੁ ਸੋਈ ਭਲਾ ਮਨਿ ਲੇਤਾ ਮੁਕਤਾ ॥

Jo Thumh Karahu Soee Bhalaa Man Laethaa Mukathaa II

One who accepts whatever You do as good - that mind is liberated.

(Raag Bilaaval: Guru Arjan Dev Ang 809 Line)

Acceptance is an attitude which is cultivated over a period of time and goes through a range of stages which begin with resistance and avoidance, moving through curiousity, tolerance understanding and finally friendship. Acceptance allows us to be compassionate to ourselves. Acceptance means, acceptance of what is happening to "us", as in acceptance of current situation, thoughts, sensations and emotions which is in contrast to acceptance of the person to whom it's happening, therefore taking a kinder and self-compassionate attitude towards oneself.

The cultivation of acceptance begins with stopping to make things "different, and simply being present in the here and now of life experience. The acceptance of external factors ultimately matures into the acceptance of that which is being experienced by the individual with a sense of openness and kindness and it is this attitude of acceptance of one self that matures into self-compassion, which further flourishes towards a non-judgemental less critical and compassionate being. The change from resistance to acceptance allows space to change.

Hukam, responsibility and blame

Life consists of continuous experience that which can be viewed as either pleasant and pleasurable, or unpleasant and suffering or neutral. When one experiences suffering, the tendency is to avoid the experience, suppress the experience, distract oneself from the experience or blame another, yet when one experience pleasure, the tendency is to "hold" or grasp the experience, prevent it from changing and the onus on oneself for creating the expereince. Gurmat views both pleasure and suffering as transient experiences of life, and emphasizes that one's own ego-bound actions lead to both pleasure and suffering, which also result in binding the individualized consciousness to the endless cycle of birth, life, death and rebirth.

ਮਾਇਆ ਕਿਸ ਨੋ ਆਖੀਐ ਕਿਆ ਮਾਇਆ ਕਰਮ ਕਮਾਇ ॥
ਦੁਖਿ ਸੁਖਿ ਏਹੁ ਜੀਉ ਬਧੁ ਹੈ ਹਉਮੈ ਕਰਮ ਕਮਾਇ ॥

Maaeiaa Kis No Aakheeai Kiaa Maaeiaa Karam Kamaae II
Dhukh Sukh Eaehu Jeeo Badhh Hai Houmai Karam Kamaae II

What is called Maya? What does Maya do?
Being bound in suffering and pleasure, acting in ego.
                                        (Sri Raag Guru Amar Das Ang:67)

Gurmat explains that as everything that is, exists within Hukam and unfolds according to Hukam, ultimate responsibility rests with Existence itself.

However, through ignorance ones' ego-bound actions create the circumstances and results of actions that bind the individualized consciousness in pain and pleasure.

Gurmat lays emphasis on taking personal responsibility of recognizing the role of the ego-complex within the back drop of existence. Recognizing oneself, as form, under-standing, location in time and space and the circumstances one find themselves in, are all within Hukam. This acceptance of self and circumstances allows one to cultivate a kinder and compassionate approach in addition to providing "personal space" for responding mindfully rather than being conditioned to react automatically.

          natt naaraaein mehalaa 5 dhupadhae
          ik oa(n)kaar sathigur prasaadh II
          oulaahano mai kaahoo n dheeou II
          man meet(h) thuhaaro keeou II1II rehaao II

aagiaa maan jaan sukh paaeiaa sun sun naam t'huhaaro
jeeou II

eehaa(n) oohaa har thum hee thum hee eihu gur thae
ma(n)thra dhrirreeou II1II

jab thae jaan paaee eaeh baathaa thab kusal khaem sabh
thheeou II

saadhhasa(n)g naanak paragaasiou aan naahee rae
beeou II2II1II2II

Raag Nat Naaraayan, Fifth Mehla, Du-Paday:

*One Universal Creator God. By the Grace of The True
Guru:*

I don't blame anyone else.

Whatever You do is sweet to my mind. II1IIPauseII

*Understanding and obeying Your Order, I have found
peace; hearing, listening to Your Name, I live.*

*Here and hereafter, You, only You. The Guru has
implanted this Mantra within me. II1II*

*Since I came to realize this, I have been blessed with total
peace and tranquility.*

*In the Saadh Sangat, the Company of the self-realised,
this has been revealed to Nanak, and now, there is no
other for him at all. II2II1II2II*

(Guru Arjan Dev Ji 978)

Forgetting that Existence is ultimately responsible for
all it is, and taking responsibility as a separate entity binds
the ego-complex within duality, which inevitably, leads to
psychological distress, feelings of isolation and helplessness.

ਹਮ ਕੀਆ ਹਮ ਕਰਹਗੇ ਹਮ ਮੂਰਖ ਗਾਵਾਰ ॥
ਕਰਨੈ ਵਾਲਾ ਵਿਸਰਿਆ ਦੂਜੈ ਭਾਇ ਪਿਆਰੁ ॥
ਮਾਇਆ ਜੇਵਡੁ ਦੁਖੁ ਨਹੀ ਸਭਿ ਭਵਿ ਥਕੇ ਸੰਸਾਰੁ ॥
ਗੁਰਮਤੀ ਸੁਖੁ ਪਾਈਐ ਸਚੁ ਨਾਮੁ ਉਰ ਧਾਰਿ ॥੩॥

Ham Keeaa Ham Karehagae Ham Moorakh Gaavaar II
Karanai Vaalaa Visariaa Dhoojai Bhaae Piaar II
Maaeiaa Jaevadd Dhukh Nehee Sabh Bhav Thhakae
Sansaar II
Guramathee Sukh Paaeeai Sach Naam Our Dhhaar II3II

"I have done this, and I will do that"-I am an idiotic fool for saying this!

I have forgotten the Doer of all; I am caught in the love of duality.

There is no pain as great as the pain of Maya; it drives people to wander all around the world, until they become exhausted.

Through the Guru's Teachings, peace is found, with the True Name enshrined in the heart. ||3||

(Sri Raag Guru Amar Das Ang:39)

The tendency to identify oneself with the content of the mind, body and emotion (ego-complex) is the result of an underdeveloped intellect, also known as Ahambudh, egoic-intellect. The dominant fused ego-complex binds the individualised consciousness (jeev) to their actions and the consequences of their actions. Therefore, actions carried out as ego-complex, with sense of ownership result in karmic consequences attached to that ego-complex.

ਅਹੰਬੁਧਿ ਸੁਚਿ ਕਰਮ ਕਰਿ ਇਹ ਬੰਧਨ ਬੰਧਾਨੀ ॥੭॥

Ahanbudhh Such Karam Kar Eih Bandhhan Bandhhaanee ||7||

He may perform religious deeds, but his mind is egotistical, and he is bound by these bonds. ||7||

(Raag Gauri: Guru Arjan Dev Ang 242)

ਦੁਖਿ ਸੁਖਿ ਏਹੁ ਜੀਉ ਬਧੁ ਹੈ ਹਉਮੈ ਕਰਮ ਕਮਾਇ ॥

Dhukh Sukh Eaehu Jeeo Badhh Hai Houmai Karam Kamaae ||

These beings are bound by pleasure and pain; they do their deeds in egotism.

(Sri Raag: Guru Amar Das Ang 67)

Self-image in Oneness

Psychological suffering has many components, one being self-image and self-concept. Self-image can either bring harmony and self-acceptance, or be the source of distress, suffering and non-acceptance. When our self-image is dictated by others, by society, religions, and popular culture, it can be the source of much anguish and pain.

Gurmat provides a foundational understanding which can significantly contribute to cultivating self-image and eliminate external triggers for suffering.

Self-image is how *one* perceives oneself. Self-image is one side of the coin and is significantly influenced by the worldview through which one is conditioned and in which one is conditioned. The other side of this coin is self-esteem, a personal evaluation of one and appraisal of one's worth. Both self-image and self-esteem are essential components of the ego-complex, Haumai ("I" amness") and ahamkara (what, who "I" am, "I"-amness creator").

The are three components of self-esteem competence, worthiness and self-evaluation, all which feed into self concept which is defined as "the individual's belief about himself or herself, including their attributes, attributes and who and what the self is".

Without going into the current theories of self-development, personality and self-esteem, suffice to note that how one perceives oneself is dependent on how one is taught to perceive oneself. To illustrate this point, consider the dominant Judeo-Christian cultural norm, whereby human beings are alive to endure suffering, expelled from "paradise" and in which women are held responsible for this "sin". The self-image of an individual brought up within this paradigm be that of a separate entity, a "sinner", whose role in life is to get back into the good books of some other worldly "God" figure.

The self-image cultivated within a worldview of interconnected Oneness, which is fearless, hate-less, timelessness and values compassion, forgiveness and optimism over anger, hate and fear significantly influences one's self-concept, self-esteem and consequently self-worth. This together with an understanding of the essential nature of reality provides a healthy and safe framework for self-growth of a healthy ego focused on its self-actualization while maintaining mental, physical, emotional health and wellbeing.

ਆਤਮ ਰਾਮੁ ਰਾਮੁ ਹੈ ਆਤਮ ਹਰਿ ਪਾਈਐ ਸਬਦਿ ਵੀਚਾਰਾ ਹੇ ॥੭॥

Aatham Raam Raam Hai Aatham Har Paaeeai Sabadh Veechaaraa Hae ||7||

Atma is Parmatma Paratma is Atma, contemplating the Shabad, the One is found.

(Raag Maaroo: Guru Nanak Dev Ang 1030)

Ethics and mental health

Ethics are contained in the "Rehat", or personal lifestyle of a follower of Gurmat teachings, it is the discipline or practical ethical framework of a person's lifestyle. This lifestyle is foundational for the cultivation of healthy mental states. Ethics are misunderstood as the rules and regulations surrounding belief systems and religions. Ethics are ones' own personal principles that govern behavior or the conducting of an activity, they are considered as one of the most valuable psychological gift to oneself, others and the environment. Gurmat asserts personal ethics are cultivated through the practice of Symran, Naam symran and selflessness. Ethics begin with "do no harm", including no harm to oneself. The more profound harm one can do to oneself, is not to recognize their essential nature and thus, be ignorant about the interconnectedness and the sacred dimension of both oneself and everything else.

Ethical dissonance refers to the inconsistency between

one's unethical behavior and the need to maintain a moral self-image.

The results ofthe current unethical predatory capitalist model are evident in the damage and pollution of most life-systems in the world, including the air, water, food, the ground, and now even space with electromagnetic radiation. Ethical living is fundamental to ones' mental health, and impact of unethical living is destructive at every level, beginning with oneself. Ethical living releases one from the psychological pressure including inner conflicts, paranoia, fear and self-harm.

In a climate when politicians, bankers, celebrities, religious leaders and institutions are immersed in unethical actions, creating bogus wars, false flags, destroying nations, displacing millions across the globe, decimating indigenous communities and most importantly, the war on freedom of thought has raised awareness of what ethical living is composed of.

Ethics are the third marker in the process of transpersonal development per Gurmat. Dedicated and consistent practice of Symran (mindfulness) will inevitably take individual through positive emotional markers that begin with contentment, moving to compassion and act as the catalyst that awaken one to personal ethics based one experience and not on conditioned behavior.

The need to be "green" and eco-friendly is the natural development of human being and function, knowing something feels "wrong" or uncomfortable to oneself. This is the feedback mechanism of one innate ethical compass, which motivates change in understanding and consequently, behaviour. Maintaining behavior when it feels uncomfortable promotes mental instability, anxiety and depression. The fundamental of ethics is to treat others (life) as one would wish to be treated themselves.

Gurmat provides a post conventional approach to ethics based on love rather than fear, compassion rather than anger or guilt and forgiveness instead of retaliation. Ethical living has immediate and far reaching effects on health and welling. It begins with healing our mind by resolving inner conflicts, which provides the psychological "space" to gradually fostering qualities of acceptance, care, kindness, forgiveness and authenticity amongst others.

Gurmat recognized the universal psychological and spiritual principal, our thoughts create our reality; what one sows is what one reaps. In other words, what one intends for another, is first created in oneself. For example, if one wishes to share love with another, it must first be present in oneself before it can be offered to others. Before projecting anger at another, it needs to manifest within oneself. Our thoughts and intention create our realities, and our subjective experiences, pleasant, unpleasant or neutral.

ਆਪੇ ਬੀਜਿ ਆਪੇ ਹੀ ਖਾਹੁ ॥

Aapae Beej Aapae Hee Khaahu ||

You shall harvest what you plant.

(Guru Nanak Dev Jap: 4)

Ethical living begins with "right worldview", knowing the nature of reality, its interconnectedness and our place in it and develops from there towards a more conscious approach to our thoughts, speech, actions and allows the healing our emotional residue from past unethical actions.

ਮਨ ਬਚ ਕ੍ਰਮ ਪ੍ਰਭੁ ਏਕੁ ਧਿਆਏ ॥
ਸਰਬ ਫਲਾ ਸੋਈ ਜਨੁ ਪਾਏ ॥੬॥

Man Bach Kram Prabh Eaek Dhhiaaeae ||
Sarab Falaa Soee Jan Paaeae ||6||

One who meditates on the One in thought, word and deed
- that humble being receives the fruits of all rewards. ||6||

(Raag Suhi Guru Arjan Dev Ang:760)

The awareness towards ethical living develops as a gradual process through meditation practice, which over time and practice, integrates into a wholesome and healthy sense of "self", with greater awareness of thoughts, words and actions beyond the imprisoned, confined and restricted ego-based living.

ਹੰਸੁ ਹੇਤੁ ਲੋਭੁ ਕੋਪੁ ਚਾਰੇ ਨਦੀਆ ਅਗਿ ॥
ਪਵਹਿ ਦਝਹਿ ਨਾਨਕਾ ਤਰੀਐ ਕਰਮੀ ਲਗਿ ॥੨॥

Hans Haeth Lobh Kop Chaarae Nadheeaa Ag II
Pavehi Dhajhehi Naanakaa Thareeai Karamee Lag II2II
Cruelty, material attachment, greed and anger are the four
   rivers of fire.
Falling into them, one is burned, O Nanak! One is saved
   only by holding tight to ethical actions. II2II

(Raag Maajh Guru Nanak Dev Ang:147)

Gurmat recognizes four "fires" or energies as psychological states which result in unethical living, and are destructive to oneself, others and the environment.

1. The fire of cruelty, violence and uncompassion
2. The fire of greed, access accumulation of wealth, power, presitige and status
3. The fire of attachment, a driving force behind all the other fires
4. The fire of anger, resentment and revenge

Each of the four fires create a psychological state in the individual, dominating and driving thoughts, which express themselves through words and actions.

The root of all such activities is the ego-complex, haumai. When one is ignorant of the mind (ego-complex) per Gurmat one wander in samsara (ocean of existence). Here the mind is controlled and driven by transient and disturbing emotions which are related to thoughts. Over time and repetition of psychological patterns creates habits that subside into and are stored as imprints in one's ground consciousness throughout one's many lives, arising again when conditions prevail. Habitual psychological patterns cause one to repeat and intensify destructive and unhealthy behaviour that ripens as karma. Gurmat asserts it is possible to become free of all habitual patterns by recognizing the mind/ego-complex and its patterns, so one can step beyond those patterns.

ਹੇ ਜਨਮ ਮਰਣ ਮੂਲੰ ਅਹੰਕਾਰੰ ਪਾਪਾਤਮਾ ॥

Hae Janam Maran Moolan Ahankaaran Paapaathamaa ||

O egotism, you are the root of birth and death and the cycle of reincarnation; you are the very source of unethical living.

(Salok Sehshritee: Guru Arjan Dev Ang 1358)

Sahej – equanimity – harmonious and optimum psycho-spiritual health

ਮਨੁ ਤਨੁ ਹਰਿਆ ਸਹਜਿ ਸੁਭਾਏ ॥
ਨਾਨਕ ਨਾਮਿ ਰਹੇ ਲਿਵ ਲਾਏ ॥

Manu tanu hariaa sahaj subhaae ||
Nanak naam rahe liv laae ||

The mind and body become rejuvenated through Sahej (Of those who) O Nanak! Remain absorbed in the Naam (Presence)

(SGGS 1173)

Sahejavasta defines the psychological state of internal harmony and optimum psycho-spiritual health, experienced as inner and outer balance, mental peace and unity. It is a "spontaneous and self-creating" psychological state different to "normal" states which tend to focus on effort to create happiness. Sahej is a natural state of homeostatic, a self-regulation system. It is ever present, however, our constant craving for happiness by wishing for "things to be different" prevents us from cultivating this natural state. It is characterised as a state of non-dual existence within a world of duality, Sahej is the product of harmonising the psychological states which directly impact the health of the body and sense of wellbeing. Gurmat teachings are replete with practices which lead to Sahejavasta, as well as descriptions of this state of optimum health and wellness.

gourree mehalaa 5 ll
gur kaa sabadh ridh a(n)thar dhhaarai ll
pa(n)ch janaa sio sa(n)g nivaarai ll
dhas ei(n)dhree kar raakhai vaas ll
thaa kai aathamai hoe paragaas ll1ll
aisee dhrirrathaa thaa kai hoe ll
jaa ko dhaeiaa maeiaa prabh soe ll1ll rehaao ll
saajan dhusatt jaa kai eaek samaanai ll
jaethaa bolan thaethaa giaanai ll
jaethaa sunanaa thaethaa naam ll
jaethaa paekhan thaethaa dhhiaan ll2ll
sehajae jaagan sehajae soe ll
sehajae hothaa jaae s hoe ll
sehaj bairaag sehajae hee hasanaa ll
sehajae choop sehajae hee japanaa ll3ll
sehajae bhojan sehajae bhaao ll
sehajae mittiou sagal dhuraao ll
sehajae hoaa saadhhoo sa(n)g ll
sehaj miliou paarabreham nisa(n)g ll4ll
sehajae grih mehi sehaj oudhaasee ll
sehajae dhubidhhaa than kee naasee ll
jaa kai sehaj man bhaeiaa ana(n)dh ll
thaa ko bhaettiaa paramaana(n)dh ll5ll
sehajae a(n)mrith peeou naam ll
sehajae keeno jeea ko dhaan ll
sehaj kathhaa mehi aatham rasiaa ll
thaa kai sa(n)g abinaasee vasiaa ll6ll

sehajae aasan asathhir bhaaeiaa ||
sehajae anehath sabadh vajaaeiaa ||
sehajae run jhunakaar suhaaeiaa ||
thaa kai ghar paarabreham samaaeiaa ||7||
sehajae jaa ko pariou karamaa ||
sehajae gur bhaettiou sach dhharamaa ||
jaa kai sehaj bhaeiaa so jaanai ||
naanak dhaas thaa kai kurabaanai ||8||3||

Gauree, Fifth Mehla:
Those who implant the Word of the Guru's Shabad within
    their hearts
cut their connections with the five passions.
They keep the ten organs under their control;
their awarenessis enlightened. ||1||
They alone acquire such stability,whom God blesses with
    His Mercy and Grace. ||1||Pause||
Friend and foe are one and the same to them.
Whatever they speak is wisdom.
Whatever they hear is the Naam
Whatever they see is consciousness (awareness). ||2||
They awaken in peace and poise; they sleep in peace and
    poise.
That which is meant to be, automatically happens.
In peace and poise, they remain detached; in peace and
    poise, they laugh.
In peace and poise, they remain silent; in peace and poise,
    they chant. ||3||
In peace and poise they eat; in peace and poise they love.
The illusion of duality is easily and totally removed.
They naturally join the Saadh Sangat, the Society of the
    Holy.
In peace and poise, they meet and merge with the
    Supreme. ||4||
They are at peace in their homes, and they are at peace
    while detached.
In peace, their bodies' duality is eliminated.
Bliss comes naturally to their minds.
They meet the Oneness, the Embodiment of Supreme
    Bliss. ||5||

In peaceful poise, they drink in the Ambrosial Nectar of the Naam.
In peace and poise, they give to the poor.
Their awareness is nutured with wisdom.
The Imperishable consciouness abides with them. ||6||
In peace and poise, they assume the unchanging position.
In peace and poise, the unstruck vibration of the Shabad resounds.
In peace and poise, the celestial bells resound.
Within them, the Supreme Essence prevades. ||7||
With intuitive ease, they merge in oneness, according to their karma.
With intuitive ease, they meet with the Guru, in the true Dharma.
Those who know, attain the poise of intuitive peace.
Slave Nanak is a sacrifice to them. ||8||3|

The experience of Sehaj avasta s conveyed in multiple expressions each conveying as aspect of the experience: "Samadhi", "turia-avastha", "chautha pad", "amar pad", "param pad", "maha-sukh", "param anand", "dasam duar", "anand", "sach khand", "jivan-mukti" and "sehaj samadh".

salok ma 3 ||
sehajae sukh suthee sabadh samaae ||
aapae prabh mael lee gal laae ||
dhubidhhaa chookee sehaj subhaae ||
a(n)thar naam vasiaa man aae ||
sae ka(n)t(h) laaeae j bha(n)n gharraae ||
naanak jo dhhur milae sae hun aan milaae ||1||
Salok, Third Mehla:
She sleeps in intuitive peace and poise, absorbed in the Word of the Shabad.
God hugs her close in His Embrace, and merges her into Himself.
Duality is eradicated with intuitive ease.
Naam comes to abide in her mind.

*He hugs close in His Embrace those who shatter and
reform their beings.*
*O Nanak, those who are predestined to meet Oneness,
come and meerge inOneness. ||1||*
(Guru Amar Daas Ji in Raag Saarang on Pannaa 1247)

Accepting death and mental health

Fear of loss of life is the root cause of all fears. This fear
is triggered because of a threat of physical death and, when
the threat is to ones' mental constructs, i.e.ego-complex. In
both situations, the root of fear is loss of "self".

On closer inspection to ones' experience in the present
moment, there is recognition of constant change, continuous
"loss" of one moment, to be replaced with another.
Understanding reality to be birth, growth and death inevitable
helps accept own mortality and thus reduces fear. Gurmat
considers that the acceptance of death is essential to mental
health, which in turn impact physical health because of the
mind body connection or psycho-physiology.

ਅਸਥਿਰੁ ਚੀਤੁ ਮਰਨਿ ਮਨੁ ਮਾਨਿਆ ॥

Asathhir Cheeth Maran Man Maaniaa ||
*His consciousness becomes permanently stable, and his
mind accepts death.*
(Raag Raamkali Dakhni: Guru Nanak Dev Ang 932)

What do you know about death and dying?
What have you done to prepare for your death?
When did you begin?
Rather than run away from that which is inevitable,
cultivating awareness of ones' own mortality can be of
profound value towards a process of acceptance and
recognition of the play underway, and your role within this
changing existence. Life, is this moment now, its s a gift to
cultivate ones' own path of self-discovery, inner transformation, growth and self-actualization.

What have you done to have this life? Everything we possess, from the food we eat, clothes that we wear and everything in between must be earned and paid for, yet, whom did you pay for this life, for your health and faculties? Life is beyond price and an invaluable gift which begins with an in breath and ends with an out breath, all the wealth in the world can not add an extra breath when our time is up. This opportunity is unique and will not come again. It is an opportunity to live life and know oneself.

Gurmat offers hope even at the last breath.

soohee ||
jo dhin aavehi so dhin jaahee ||
karanaa kooch rehan thhir naahee ||
sa(n)g chalath hai ham bhee chalanaa ||
dhoor gavan sir oopar maranaa ||1||
kiaa thoo soeiaa jaag eiaanaa ||
thai jeevan jag sach kar jaanaa ||1|| rehaao ||
jin jeeo dheeaa s rijak a(n)baraavai ||
sabh ghatt bheethar haatt chalaavai ||
kar ba(n)dhigee shhaadd mai maeraa ||
hiradhai naam samhaar savaeraa ||2||
janam siraano pa(n)thh n savaaraa ||
saa(n)jh paree dheh dhis a(n)dhhiaaraa ||
kehi ravidhaas nidhaan dhivaanae ||
chaethas naahee dhuneeaa fan khaanae ||3||2||

Soohee:
That day which comes, that day shall go.
You must march on; nothing remains stable.
Our companions are leaving, and we must leave as well.
We must go far away. Death is hovering over our heads. ||1||
Why are you asleep? Wake up, you ignorant fool!
You believe that your life in the world is unchanging. ||1|| Pause||
The One who gave you life shall also provide you with nourishment.

In each and every heart, He runs His shop.
Meditate and renounce your egotism and self-conceit.
Within your heart, contemplate the Naam sometime. ||2||
Your life has passed away, but you have not arranged your
path.
Evening has set in, and soon there will be darkness on all
sides.
Says Ravi Daas, O ignorant mad-man, don't you realize,
that this world is the house of death?! ||3||2|

CHAPTER THREE

The Gurmat Model of a Human Being

The Gurmat Model of a Human being

The Gurmat model of human being is a multi-layered, energetic phenomenon experienced as a tri-dimensional psycho-physical-spiritual being, which begins with Atma – embodied consciousness or the spiritual self (SGGS 441). However, this spiritual self is not an individual soul or self, but part of the cosmic consciousness, the conscious-ness which unifies all diversity. Atma is the wave upon the ocean of Consciousness known as Parmatman, Atma, Self, Ek, Akal Purekh or Braham; (One pervasive unchanging Presence ever-existent, unfolding through the impermanence of creating, sustaining and destruction, beyond time, fear, hate, birth and self-existing) are indistinguishable.

According to Eastern psychology and philosophy, the human body is composed of five layers or sheaths called "koshas". These five sheaths represent the various levels of our being and construct what we consider to be our experience and are divided into the following.

"Annamaya kosha" is the action body, the physical or food sheath and is dependent on food, air and water. It provides strength and stability to the physical body. The five sense organs are part of annamaya kosha and are also connected to the conscious mind, particularly in its sense gratification phase the mind takes on the characteristics of annamaya kosha.

"Pranayama kosha" is the energy (life-force) or feeling body which also provides energy to the physical Anamaya kosha. According to yoga including Kundalini yoga, the Pranayama kosha is described in terms of the three main energy channels of Susmanan, Ida and pingla which, in turn, are part of the seven Chakras system.

"Maanmaya kosha" is the mind-body complex responsible for ones' experience in life, it relates to perception which is processed because of the sensory information provided through the five sense organs.

"Vigyanamaya kosha" is the intuitive body sheath and is concerned with gyan or inner wisdom, vi-gyan, knowing that which was unknown before. However, this sheath is normally "awakened", fully functioning under specific states of consciousness known as "Chitta", the seat of conscious experience. Meditation, to train awareness on single pointedness specifically, is a prerequisite for awakening this sheath.

Anandmaya kosha is the ultimate experience of being human, a non-dual blissful pure consciousness experience. Ananda is the ultimate joy sought after by all human beings, experienced by transcending duality as a non-dual ecstatic experience. However, while everyone is searching for Anand, Gurmat asserts that without the teaching and guidance of a Guru, Self-realised enlightened or ego-transcended teacher, one is unable to achieve this state.

ਆਨੰਦੁ ਆਨੰਦੁ ਸਭੁ ਕੋ ਕਹੈ ਆਨੰਦੁ ਗੁਰੂ ਤੇ ਜਾਣਿਆ ॥

Aanandh Aanandh Sabh Ko Kehai Aanandh Guroo Thae Jaaniaa ॥

Bliss, bliss - everyone talks of bliss; bliss is known only
through the guru.

(Guru Amar Das SGGS 927)

The five koshas are arranged into three bodies, namely, Ashtula Sareer (gross physical body), Sukhsham Sareer (subtle body – internal psychological appratus) and Karana Sareer (causal body).

The Ashtula Sareer or gross body is the physical body which consists of five elements; earth (solid), water (liquid), fire (plasma), air (gas) and space,and is subject to six modifications of the body, existence, birth, growth, change, decay and death. The physical body is the manifestation of the other two bodies. "Annamaya" includes the physical manifestation of Pranamaya kosha, or the energy –feeling sheathin the physical body. This body is dependent on nourishment obtained from physical food, water and air. Upon death, the physical body disintegrates into its five constituent elements.

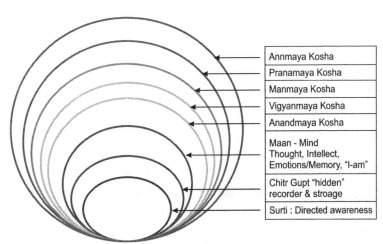

The physical body is entangled within existence through ignorance. Ignorance clouds the real from the unreal, the transient from the permanent, and gives rise to judgement either as attraction or aversion, which in turn motivates the actions.

It is this ignorance that binds the ego-complex to its actions and thus the consequences of karma attached to those actions.

The mind is asleep and resides in ignorance, not knowing. This ignorance is the inability to distinguish the transient from the permanent, and thus the mind as I-am-ness or Ahamkara, is bound to making judgement towards what it perceives as "pleasant" and repel that it judges to be "unpleasant", giving rise to actions and karma.

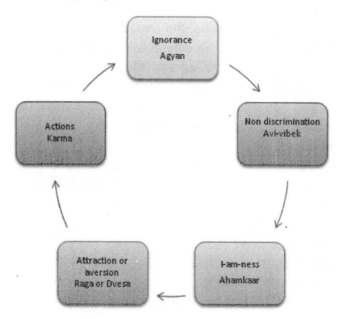

Ignorance (Agyan) → non-discrimination between real and unreal (Aviveka) → I-am-ness (Ahamkaar) → attraction and aversion (raga-dvesha) → actions (karma)

Ignorance traps the mind within this repetitive cognitive

cycles and consequently, trapping the mind within the cycle of reincarnation. The sukhsham sareer or subtle body is composed of nineteen principles (Tattvas), viz., five Gyana Indriyas or sense-organs of knowledge, five Karma Indriyas or organs of action, five Pranas or vital airs, Manas or thoughts, Buddhi or intellect, Chitta or memory/mental substance and Ahamkara or I am-creator.

The subtle body contains the psychological or inner-psychological-apparatus, "Antakaran". It is the name given collectively to the four faculties of our Mind; I-am-creator, Chitta (feeling emotions), Mind (thoughts) and intelligence (discrimination). There is no term in the Western language for "Antakaran".

As the name implies, the causal body is the cause of other two bodies, it is "undifferentiated form" which has no other function being the seed for the other two bodies. It is characterized as "emptiness", "ignorance", and "darkness". It is also identified as the container or storehouse for "sanskars", or impression of experiences from previous experiences.

The mind is a continuum of the matter, it is the interfacing instrument between the external world of phenomena on one side and consciousness on the other. There is a direct mind-body interaction and connection; our mental states have a direct impact on our physical body recognised now as psycho-physiology. Over the past decade or so, western science has begun to recognize that psychosocial factors can directly influence both physiologic function and health outcomes; However, Western medicine has completely failed to move beyond the "biomedical" model.[27,]

The biomedical theory of disease grew around the conviction that most diseases are caused by invaders from the outside 'micro organisms or germs', genetics or inflammation and is both incomplete and distorted in its approach to health and wellbeing. Limitations of the biomedical model include, the mind-body duality, in which the mind is separate, and independent from the body; the ignorance about the influence of our psychological states on the physiology of the body; the cause of illness is external, i.e. germs, virus or bacteria, genetics or inflammation, without any consideration of the mental or emotional states on health and wellbeing; The bio medical model focuses on treating the disease independent of the patient, without any consideration on the root cause of ill health. Since the biomedical model assumes that the mind has no influence on the bodys physiology, it completely dismisses the impact of unhealthy mental states on physical body.[28,29]

In contrast to this incomplete model of health, Gurmat offers a holistic model for health and wellbeing which sees health having a physical, mental, emotional and spiritual element, and in which the body is the expression or that which is mirroring unbalance within.

Humans have the unique ability to create unhealthy physiological states which are as a direct result of their mental states, such as sustained stress, anger or depression. Due to disregard of the mind-body connection and ignorance about the nature of the mind in "modern"-western psychological models, there is no training available which help individuals learn about the nature of their mind and ego (Haumai) and its function in creating unhealthy physiological conditions when subjected to real or psychological threats, and importantly, how to restorebalance and homeostasis.

Unfortunately, such ignorance or avidya or agyan has manifested itself in the overwhelming presence of diseases like diabetes, coronary heart conditions, depression, cancers to mention but a few. This lack of awareness is perhaps the greatest cause of human suffering in the modern world, both in terms of propagating diseases and dividing oneself.

In the field of health psychology, the focus of research on the impact of chronic stress and health is well documented and clearly demonstrates that mental states such as stress, fear, anger and anxiety all contribute to ill health and celluar malfunction. Although research has confirmed the link between ill- health and stress, the current biomedical model is far too important to the pharmaceutical companies and related health industries and services.[30]

The Gurmat model of a human being is a multi-dimensional one, which includes consciousness within the three states of ordinary consciousness, awake state (jagrat), the dream state (supan), dreamless sleep state (sushupti):

Unconscious or hidden recorder of all thoughts, words and actions, the mind and body in its various sheaths, inseparable from natural organic trimorphic (creation, growth, death) Existence. These multi-layered model begins with consciousness.

Consciousness (Cit) consisting of four different states, the awake state (jagrat), the dream state (supan), dreamless sleep state (sushupti) and the fourth state (Turiya avasta or chauda padh)

Chitra gupt or the hidden records are regarded as the unconscious sphere, which store cognitive-behavioural impressions (sanskar) accumulated through our actions throughout life and transmigration. These impressions are created through mental (mansakh), verbal (vaashakh) and physical (sareerakh) acts, and become the "pollution" (maal) or conditioning and become the paradigm through which the individual thinks, feels and behaves. Thus, the individual is bound by habitual behavioural consequences or karma (sggs 252). This condition is described as a Manmukhi or ego facing.

The next layer is the Mind (antakaran) which consists of sensory-perceptions and thoughts (Manas), memory/ intention/emotions (Chitta), intellect/discrimination (buddhi) and I-am-creator (ahamkara).

Gurmat distinguishes different types of intelligence. For example, the intellect that can exercise acute ethical discrimination is called bibek buddhi as opposed to aham-buddhi or ego-led discrimination.

Human body – composed of three "bodies" made of five sheets or Khosas accessible as states of consciousness
Bodies means mode of experience or energetic feelings.

1. Astula Saheer – Gross body
2. Suksham saheer – Subtle body
3. Karana saheer – Causal body

Sukham Saheer contains the Antakarana – inner psychological apparatus
Antakarana or Maan (mind) is composed

1. Maan
2. Chitta
3. Buddhi
4. Ahamkaar

Jeev atma, or jiva-caitanya is the embodied human conscious-ness.

States of consciousness
1. Dreamless sleep   } Ordinary states of consciousness
2. Dream sleep
3. Awake
4. Turiya – Pure consciousness experience

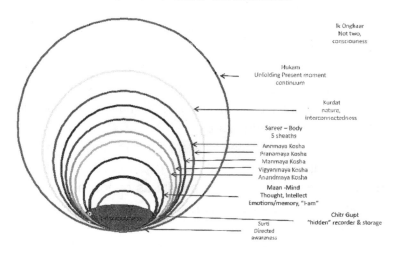

Experience of the ultimate Reality is not a matter for reason; it comes by revelation of itself through nadar (grace) and by anubhava (emotion following the experience).

Says Guru Nanak, buddhi pathi na paiai bahu chaturaiai bhai milai mani bhane which translates to "He/She is not accessible through intellect, or through mere scholarship or cleverness at argument; He/She is met, when He/She pleases, through devotion" (GG, 436).

The nature of Mind

While we all have a mind, very few of us realise that we are NOT our mind. The nature of the human mind is very subtle and difficult to understand. In Western psychology, Freud defined the structure of the personality in terms of the unconscious, preconscious, and conscious which has dominated the world of psychology across the world, setting aside thousands of years of subjective research and experience as found in the Indian traditions of Buddhism, Adviata and Sikhi. Freud, like almost all Western schools of psychology only focuses on the ego or personality and has yet to go beyond the ego to know the mind, let alone consciousness.

We are all conditioned ("maal" or mentally pollution) from birth by our language, interaction with their parents, religions,schools and society to identify with our psychological and conditioned sense of self, or Haumai (ego-complex). Haumai can be considered as a onion, layers of condition. These layers of identity can be gradually peeled away, allowing awareness from physical, mental, emotional, layers towards a clearer experienced sacred sense of self, or pure consciousness.

Gurmat considers the mind to be a subtle form of matter, made up of the same five elements found in all Existence, air (gaseous), water (liquid-fluid), fire plasma (electricity, energetic charge), earth(solid) and space, whereas, consciousness is non-corporeal. Atma is the universal life-principle, consciousness experiencing life, as "Jeev", embodied consciousness experience of human beings; It is reflected in the mind in two forms, a transcendental and phenomena. The mind or mun is a product of the five elements (tattvas) and is the psychological composite "Antakaran", a clear and knowing internal psychological instrument of "Buddhi" or intellect/discrimination, "chit" or memory/intention, "maan" or thought and Ahamkara or "I am myself-I-am-creator".

Eihu Man Panch Thath Thae Janamaa ‖
This mind is born of the five elements.
(Guru Nanak Dev 415)

The mind manifests continuously as dynamic activity which forms the interface between manifesting existence on one side and consciousness on the other, giving rise to the duality of subject and object through perception.

Consciousness through sensory awareness becomes the phenomenal aspect of consciousness, awareness of form and content which is differentiated as cognising subject, cognised object and experience of cognition, yet are fundamentally One. At the transcendental level, "Turiya", consciousness is experienced without the subject- object duality, as pure content-less awareness

The mind can be considered to have three aspects, namely perception, cognition and awareness, perception through sensory awareness, cognition as reflective awareness and consciousness as untainted awareness. Consciousness or "Brahma/Purekh" is self-manifesting, self-illuminating, content-less, unknowable as an object of cognition, yet foundational for all awareness and knowledge. It is embodied within a person (Atma), linked to the mind, manifesting as transcendental and phenomenal reflected awareness in the individualised mind.

The embodied consciousness (Jeev-Atma) is constrained by the body-mind complex (jeev) while the mind itself may be considered unconscious. The uniqueness of the "jeev" enables it to reflect consciousness such that its contents are revealed and illuminated by the embodied consciousness (Atma). Thus, the jeev becomes conscious like a light bulb illuminating the lampshade, where the light bulb may be considered as the content-less, formless, self-illuminated consciousness (Atma), and the lampshade as the mind.

Through this illumination, the mind manifests subjective experience or the phenomenal aspect of consciousness or awareness. Through this sense of subjectivity as phenomenal awareness, the mind is conditioned into binding itself with the content of its awareness, including thoughts, intellect, memory and all phenomenal activity into a false identity, or Ahamkara or (I-am-maker).

The Mind as the internal coordinating instrument is called Antakaran ("internal psychological apparatus",) or inner modes of action, which has four faculties that can be functionally distinguished into Manas (thought, sensorial mind), Chitta (memory/intention, mental substance, emotion), Buddhi (discrimination / intellect), and Ahamkara (Sense of "I"-am-maker" pronounced Ahamkara). Antakaran is the composite of awareness and response system. In contrast, it is important to note there is no corresponding term within Western vocabulary for Antakaran which also goes to demonstrate the progress made in Indic consciousness tradition in knowing the mind

Antakaran refers to the "internal psychological apparatus", it is important to explore the meaning of Antakaran in relations to Indriyas (sense organs and action organs) and explore the individual nature of "Mann", "Buddhi", "Chitta" and "Ahamkara". The Antakaran perceives through five sense organs (Gyan Indiria) and instructs the five organs of action (Karam Indiria): the organ of speech, the hands, the legs, the organ of procreation, and the organ of evacuation

The four components of Antakaran, Manas,Chit, Buddhi and Ahamkara and are distinguished as follows:

"Manas" is the central processing system, normally subdivided into two parts, Manas (thought) and Chitta. The term "Chitta" means mind-substance, refers to the quality of mental processes it represents an emotional-mental (heart-mind) component of one's mindset, or state of mind.

"Buddhi" is the executive system, the intellect, the facility to discriminate. According to Gurmat, "Buddhi" has several variations depending on its maturity. "Ahambudh", also referred to as "chapal buddhi" (the unstable intellect), "buddhi bikar" (polluted intellect), "malin buddhi" (turbid intellect), "nibal buddhi" (weak intellect), "durmat buddhi" (perverse intellect), and "phanin buddhi" (the deluding intellect) which is ego-centric, always self-interest discrimination or intellect.

This discriminatory faculty matures through contemplative and ethical practices into Bibek buddhi, the ability to discriminate without ego-centricity, self-interest, and within internal ethical boundaries. This subtle sense of discrimination helps one to know the difference between "Sat" (Reality, unchanging, permanent) and "Asat"(falsehood, changing, temporary) or correct and incorrect.

> Antar lobh halak dukh bhareei bin bibek bharmaai ||1||:
> *(The man with Haumai attaches to Maya) the great ailment of the rabid disease of greed is within him. Without Bibek (discriminating intellect), he wanders around (like a rabid dog) ||1||*
>
> (SGGS 1132)

"Bibek buddhi" is also known as"sar-buddhi" (the essential intellect), "tat buddhi" (the essential intellect), "bimal" or "nirmal buddhi" (unclouded, clear intellect), "bal buddhi" (powerful intellect), "mati buddhi" (the counselling intellect) and "sudh buddhi" (pure intellect).

> Bibek budhi beechaar gurmukh gur sabad khin khin har nit chave:
> *With Bibek-Budhi, the Gurmukhs contemplate the Gur-Shabad; each and every instant, they continually speak of the One (ever present).*
>
> (SGGS 1114)

"Chitta"; Memory, intention and feeling. "Chitta" is derived from the word "Cit" or consciousness, it is considered as the universal medium or mental substance in which the mind functions. "Chitta", is responsible for the Vritties which can be translated as "thought-waves", "vortex", "waves" or "ripples", they give rise to emotional states, moods, which impact behaviour, conduct, activity etc.

Vrtties is a process taking place as modification of that mental substance, like waves arise from the surface of the ocean; Vrittis arise from the surface of the mind-ocean.

ਜਿਚਰੁ ਇਹੁ ਮਨੁ ਲਹਰੀ ਵਿਚਿ ਹੈ ਹਉਮੈ ਬਹੁਤੁ ਅਹੰਕਾਰੁ ॥

Jichar Eihu Man Leharee Vich Hai Houmai Bahuth Ahankaar ||

As long as his mind is disturbed by waves, its caught in Houmai (I-am-myself) and Ahamkara(I-am-creator).

(Guru Amar Das Ang:1247)

ਉਰਝਿ ਰਹਿਓ ਬਿਖਿਆ ਕੈ ਸੰਗਾ ॥
ਮਨਹਿ ਬਿਆਪਤ ਅਨਿਕ ਤਰੰਗਾ ॥੧॥

Ourajh Rehiou Bikhiaa Kai Sangaa ||
Manehi Biaapath Anik Tharangaa ||1||

Entangled in poisonous associations;
The mind is troubled by so many waves. ||1||

(Guru Arjan Dev Ang:759)

"Ahamkara": The experience of personal identity or the self-sense is known as aham, which is equivalent to 'I' in the English language, while "kar" can be translated as "continuous form", thus Ahamkara, is translated into "I-am-creator" or "I-am-ness". Ahamkara is our internal, dynamic identity system creator. This system is not dissimilar to the nervous system, the circulatory system and other systems that exist in the human body, apart from being psychological as opposed to physical. Our conditioned mind consisting of thoughts, memories, discrimination, and intention, as ego or Haumai. One inherent quality of our ego is desire, an innate thirst seeking satisfaction, and engages in constant activity that confirms and reconfirms its own existence, its "I-am-ness" or Ahamkara as the creator of I-amness.

Hau, can be translated as the psychological identity or

"ego". Self-identification as a separate and individual existence as "I-am-myself", "Ahamkara"is the identification or attachment to one's Haumai and represents the attribute-grasping "trisanaa" or craving element of our identity.

"Ahamkara" is also expressed as specialness, self-obsession, self-conceit, self-centeredness, self-adulation, self-pride all underlying a need to exert permanence and security. Ahamkara represents the attributes of haumai.

"Ahamkara" is experienced consciously and un-consciously as a form of "specialness" or self-referencing, a continuous creation of a false identity of self-importance, overtly or implied. This specialness can be either positive through care, attention and nurturing, or negatively through lack of attention, care or adequate nurturing.

This sense of self, "Ahamkara", is a continuous identity making system which inherently feel unsecure, incomplete and deficient, thus seeks sense of security and permanence through attachments. This dynamic sense of grasping or craving (trisanaa) in turn give rise to emotions, which are bipolar in their nature, "Sukh" and "Dukh", absence of suffering and suffering respectively.

Through desires and attachments individuals develop a false sense of self by identifying themselves with external objects, including body, youth, objects, and so on. The continuous grasping nature of ahamkara as attachments, attractions and repulsion is termed as mental affliction, or "Klesha". (see Klesha)

"Ahamkara" along with constant craving, "trisanaa" are psychological malfunctioning or mental illness. This mental state is underpinned by craving, which in turn triggers the threat response system. Cravings are the uncontrolled desires that direct our awareness from present moment into thoughts relating to the cravings. While most people are familiar with food cravings, most are unaware how the mind is conditioned to desire "objects" that will make one feel more fulfilled or satisfied. Cravings lead to attachments, and create our false sense of identity, and therefore lead us away from our true nature.

The nature of craving is such that is feeds our egoic sense of identity, believing ourselves to be incomplete and deficient, cravings enable us to hide, compensate or distract us from our sense of deficiencies.

ਅਹੰਕਾਰੁ ਤਿਸਨਾ ਰੋਗੁ ਲਗਾ ਬਿਰਥਾ ਜਨਮੁ ਗਵਾਵਹੇ ॥

Ahankaar Thisanaa Rog Lagaa Birathhaa Janam Gavaavehae ||

Self-conceit and craving are the disease by which you are wasting your life away in vain.

(Guru Amar Das Ang 441)

Haumai ("Hau=I, mai=me, I-am-myself" self-referencing sense of "I" or ego-complex)

Within Western or modern psychological definitions, there appears to be no clear definition about self and ego, as both terms are interchangeably jumbled. In addition, the nature of the ego, including its definition, activities and uses are all yet to be researched, discovered and understood. Professionals engaged in psychological health are more likely to use such terms, employing them across a wide spectrum of definitions, adding to the confusion between theoretical psychological constructs and experiential behavioural observations.

Eastern or ancient psychology has a history extending well over 3000 years in which the mind, consciousness and ego have been subjectively researched with practical methods to know the mind and to transcend the mental construct of Haumai or ego. The sacred texts from the traditions of

Buddhists, Hindus and Sikhs have demonstrated clear definitions in relation to the mind, consciousness and its nature.

Gurmat differentiates between hau and haumai. While "hau" represents the internal psychological sense of self or identity, or "I"-am-ness, haumai is this psychological self-identified with the physical body and self-image.

In our present state as an individual state of consciousness we tend to identify with the content of our mind, thoughts, emotions and body which give rise to the illusionary sense of separated self, Haumai. Our experience of life is one of constant change, living in a dualistic world of changing forms. This provides an innate sense of insecurity and our "haumai", attempts to stabilise itself through attachments primarily to wealth, fame, prestige or knowledge.

However, through the passage of time we discover this to be wrong, and all our attempts to create a sense of stability and security have been proven to be incorrect and wrong.In other words, just like everything else, our haumai is subject to the eternal law of change and just as the body, thought and emotions change, so does our haumai or ego-complex. Our experience of suffering is primarily causedby the haumais'attempt to stabilize or control that which cannot be controlled.

The hau or ego-complex begins as a sense of separation but over time the emphasis shifts from "I-am" to "I-am-this or that", Haumai shifting into Ahamkara, "I-am-creator" by attaching itself to attributes of being a separate self.

Gurmat considers Haumai (ego-complex) both as a necessity but also as a diseased (distorted sense of self), which operates as a continuous dynamically active psychologically complex experienced as "sense of identity".

"Haumai", "hau" mean "assertion of identity", "mai" meaning, mine, belonging to me, so, Hau-mai, is the internal self-assertion of identity.

Gurmat recognises the cyclic nature of Existence, including transmigration of embodied consciousness. It is the actions carried out in the assertion of "I-am-the doer", or Haumai which determines the transmigration of life, from one life to another.

> mehalaa 2 ||
> houmai eaehaa jaath hai houmai karam kamaahi ||
> houmai eaeee ba(n)dhhanaa fir fir jonee paahi ||
> houmai kithhahu oopajai kith sa(n)jam eih jaae ||
> houmai eaeho hukam hai paeiai kirath firaahi ||
> houmai dheeragh rog hai dhaaroo bhee eis maahi ||
> kirapaa karae jae aapanee thaa gur kaa sabadh kamaahi ||
> naanak kehai sunahu janahu eith sa(n)jam dhukh jaahi ||2||
> *Second Mehla:*
> *The nature of ego is such that people perform their actions in ego.*
> *This is the bondage of ego, that time and time again one is caught in the cycle of reincarnation.*
> *Where does ego come from? How can it be removed?*
> *Ego comes to be as a natural organic process of unfolding Existence, (Hukam), binding according to past actions.*
> *Ego is a chronic disease, but it contains its own cure as well.*
> *Throughthe Grace of Existence, one acts according to the Teachings of the Guru's.*
> *Nanak says, listen, people: in this way, suffering depart. ||2||*

Although the ego is a chronic disease, it is still an essential part of human development. Our imagined sense of me is the core of our ego believing it to be separate from everything else. Therefore, the ego develops attachments with all that is and believes it to be me "mine". The sense of my body, my thoughts, my emotions, my beliefs, my religion, my family, my possessions, reinforces this sense of duality.

As a natural part of human development,the ego has several roles and functions necessary for human function and evolution. Primarily, functions as the survival and protection control structure, used to manage and navigate lifᴄ created in the Mind.

The sense of control helps provide the ego-complex with the belief of security and stability.To reinforce this belief of security and stability, the same control structure craves attachment to thoughts, emotions, body, beliefs, objects and so on. The ego then begins to believe that this interface with Existence is who we are. It is the belief in that,the transitional mental structure as real and permanent, and through its actions,that binds the Jeev, (embodied consciousness) in the cycle of reincarnation.

> ma 3 ||
> ha(n)oumai a(n)dhar kharrak hai kharrakae kharrak vihaae ||
> ha(n)oumai vaddaa rog hai mar ja(n)mai aavai jaae ||
> jin ko poorab likhiaa thinaa sathagur miliaa prabh aae ||
> naanak gur parasaadhee oubarae houmai sabadh jalaae ||2||
>
> *Third Mehla:*
> *Ego is assailed by fear, passing life consumed by fear.*
> *Ego is such a terrible disease; one dies only to be born continuing coming and going.*
> *Those who have such pre-ordained destiny meet with Authentic Pure Consciousness experience.*
> *O Nanak, by Guru's Grace, they are redeemed; their egos are burnt away through the Word of the Shabad. ||2||*

The Haumai (ego) has several activities which help appreciate how it functions. It is occupied either by thoughts of the past, or fantasies about the future, or by telling itself stories of being a victim or a hero.This constant fusion with psychological and emotional content and inner chatter ensures that direct awareness moment by moment experience of here and now, how things are, is lost to the internal preoccupation.

Furthermore, the Haumai, (ego) believes what it thinks to be true, thoughts are never challenged therefore the ego-complex identify and fuses itself with thoughts and emotions generated. This identification, known as cognitive fusion, is usually involuntary and unconscious process and is known as "Manmukh" in Gurmat. Cognitive fusion combined with avoiding difficult emotions tend to pull one out of the present moment and into "stories" the ego tells and believes. Combined with limited compassion and self-compassion adds to the cause of suffering both, to oneself and others.

The recognition of suffering itself is the first step in understanding how to alleviate suffering. Once suffering is understood then the cause of suffering begins to reveal itself as this ego-attachment, firstly to itself, and then to specific states judged to be pleasant, unpleasant or neutral.

Insight into the causes of one's suffering and healing of suffering involves one's whole being, including intellect, cognition and emotions, which is worked through by cultivating awareness, learning to recognize the unadulterated experience in its authenticity. Symran, (Sanskrit word "simritti") and the word "Sati" in Pali are translated as mindfulness, which literally means to "remember" or re-connect, to bring back together, to harmonize (sehaj) our experience into an integrated non-dual whole Oneness.

Acceptance in awareness, or non-judgmental present moment awareness helps create the psychological space to recognize the unfolding moment by moment experience or Hukam.

The source of suffer (**Dukh**) is the fusion of our "identity" with a false sense of self, called Haumai or the ego-complex, which binds the human condition into a cyclic condition at both a psychological level and with cycles of birth, death and rebirth.

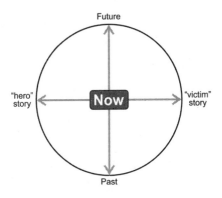

The ego-complex (mind) develops five defects:

1. It is conditioned into identifying itself with a mental construct called Haumai

   The pollution of so many births is attached to this mind and it has become pitch black (SGGS 651).

2. It is restless, unable to be here and now, but consumed with fantasising and planning the future, replaying the past, continuously jumping from one train of thoughts to another.

   ਧਾਤੁਰ ਬਾਜੀ ਸਬਦਿ ਨਿਵਾਰੇ ਨਾਮੁ ਵਸੈ ਮਨਿ ਆਈ ॥੧੨॥

   Dhhaathur Baajee Sabadh Nivaarae Naam Vasai Man Aaee ||12||

   Restrain your restless wanderings through the Shabad, and the Naam will come to dwell in your mind. ||12||
   (Raag Raamkali Guru Amar Das Ang:909)

   The tossing mind wanders in ten directions (i.e., restlessness) it needs to be pacified and restrained (sggs 685).

3. It is ignorant of itself, assuming all thoughts, beliefs and assumptions to be "facts". Thoughts are NOT facts. This ignorance separates the Haumai itself from being part of Existence, thus disconnected and ignorant of the interconnectness of Existence.

   There is ignorance and pain of doubt within, like a separating veil (i.e., veil of ignorance) between the man and God (sggs 40).

4. It is divided which manifests itself through self-stories in which the "me" is either a victim or a hero.

5. Most importantly, Haumai by default operates on self-preservation mode, automatic pilot, or absent-mindedness. Its reacts rather than responds with awareness to stimuli, real or perceived.

Gurmat considers all experiences of life to be a dream, transient and impermanent, which is no different to the experience in a dream. Although they appear to be real, upon waking they disappear. Gurmat presents the processed conditioning of the human mind and identifies the stages of development from birth right through to death.

> ma 1 ||
> pehilai piaar lagaa thhan dhudhh ||
> dhoojai maae baap kee sudhh ||
> theejai bhayaa bhaabhee baeb ||
> chouthhai piaar oupa(n)nee khaedd ||
> pa(n)javai khaan peean kee dhhaath ||
> shhivai kaam n pushhai jaath ||
> sathavai sa(n)j keeaa ghar vaas ||
> at(h)avai krodhh hoaa than naas ||
> naavai dhhoulae oubhae saah ||
> dhasavai dhadhhaa hoaa suaah ||
> geae sigeeth pukaaree dhhaah ||
> ouddiaa ha(n)s dhasaaeae raah ||

aaeiaa gaeiaa mueiaa naao ||
pishhai pathal sadhihu kaav ||
naanak manamukh a(n)dhh piaar ||
baajh guroo ddubaa sa(n)saar ||2||
First Mehla:
First, the baby loves mother's milk;
second, he learns of his mother and father;
third, his brothers, sisters-in-law and sisters;
fourth, the love of play awakens.
Fifth, he runs after food and drink;
sixth, in his sexual desire, he does not respect social
customs.
Seventh, he gathers wealth and dwells in his house;
eighth, he becomes angry, and his body is consumed.
Ninth, he turns grey, and his breathing becomes labored;
tenth, he is cremated, and turns to ashes.
His companions send him off, crying out and lamenting.
The swan of the soul takes flight, and asks which way to
go.
He came and he went, and now, even his name has died.
After he left, food was offered on leaves, and the birds
were called to come and eat.
O Nanak, the self-willed manmukhs love the darkness.
Without the Guru, the world is drowning. ||2||

Manmukh and Gurmukh

Two central terms for human existence are "Manmukh" (mindless, psychologically unhealthy, operating on automatic conditioned patterns) and "Gurmukh." (mindful, aware, present, psychologically healthy). "Maan", Mind describes a sense of self based awareness which identifies itself with the content or phenomena of awareness, such as, thoughts, emotions, sensations, body, objects and so on. This fused self exists both structurally as a sense of "I"-am-myself" or Haumai and as an activity of continuous grasping in both

subconscious and conscious attempts to
reinforce the sense of "I" or Ahamkara th
principal psychological functions which are
this activity, trapping the individual within a conditioned-false
sense of self.

Manmukh: "I-am-ness",
Identity fused with content of
the mind thoughts, emotions,
body, beliefs, desires

Gurmukh: Identity as
awareness per se

ਮਿਥਿਆ ਸੰਗਿ ਸੰਗਿ ਲਪਟਾਏ ਮੋਹ ਮਾਇਆ ਕਰਿ ਬਾਧੇ ॥
ਜਹ ਜਾਨੋ ਸੋ ਚੀਤਿ ਨ ਆਵੈ ਅਹੰਬੁਧਿ ਭਏ ਆਂਧੇ ॥੧॥

Mithhiaa Sang Sang Lapattaaeae Moh Maaeiaa Kar
Baadhhae II
Jeh Jaano So Cheeth N Aavai Ahanbudhh Bheae
Aaandhhae II1II

They are attached to falsehood; clinging to the transitory,
they are trapped in emotional attachment to Maya.
Wherever they go, they do not aware of Present Moment
Presence; they are blinded by intellectual egotism. II1II
(Guru Arjan Dev 402)

ਗੁਰਮੁਖਿ ਵਿਚਹੁ ਹਉਮੈ ਜਾਇ ॥

Guramukh Vichahu Houmai Jaae II
The Gurmukh eradicates sense of self within.

ਗੁਰਮੁਖਿ ਮੈਲੁ ਨ ਲਾਗੈ ਆਇ ॥

Guramukh Mail N Laagai Aae ||

Gurmukh is beyond psychological-conditioning.

ਗੁਰਮੁਖਿ ਨਾਮੁ ਵਸੈ ਮਨਿ ਆਇ ॥੨॥

Guramukh Naam Vasai Man Aae ||2||

Gurmukh mind becomes aware of Presence (naam) ||2||

ਗੁਰਮੁਖਿ ਕਰਮ ਧਰਮ ਸਚਿ ਹੋਈ ॥

Guramukh Karam Dhharam Sach Hoee ||

Through ethical actions, Gurmukh becomes authentic.

ਗੁਰਮੁਖਿ ਅਹੰਕਾਰੁ ਜਲਾਏਏ ਦੋਈ ॥

Guramukh Ahankaar Jalaaeae Dhoee ||

The Gurmukh burns away sense of "I-am-ness" and duality.

(Guru Amar Das Ang:230)

Through the grace of Satguru, the authentic source of enlightenment, every conditioned-self has the potential to find release from the false sense of self or "Haumai" and experience a sovereign sacred self, "Atma Parkass." Guru Nanak advocates the practice of "Naam Symran", mindful remembrance of "Shabad" or sound vibration. Through listening to the process of sound manifestation within oneself, one undergoes a process of insights as awareness develops awareness of itself as Presence, the source of enlightenment through direct experience, through the potentiality which exists within all.

"Naam Symran" and "sewa" or selflessness (without expectation of a reward to benefit to oneself) activities enable the conditioned mind to liberate itself from an anxiety and fear based experience of social existence to an all-encompassing sovereign state grounded in acceptance, unconditional love and compassion for existence, or Gurmukh state, Awareness-facing or identified with awareness or mindful.

Bin Sabadhai Naam N Paaeae Koee Gur Kirapaa Mann
Vasaavaniaa ||2||

*Without the Shabad, the Naam is not obtained. By Guru's
grace, it lives within our mind. ||2||*

(Guru Amar Das 124)

Gur Kai Sabadh Man Jeethiaa Gath Mukath Gharai Mehi
Paae ||

*Through the Word of the Guru's shabad, the mind is
conquered, and one attains the State of Liberation in
one's own home.*

(Guru Amar Das 26)

Jinee Aatham Cheeniaa Paramaatham Soee ||
*Those who becomes aware of their own awareness, are
themselves supreme.*

(Guru Nanak Dev 421)

Gurmukh is a state of mindful awareness, a realised-
self, an authentic experience of sovereign sacred existence.
This transformation is achieved through ego-transcendence,
by overcoming duality to a lived experience as a non-dual
ego-less sovereign existence.

gourree mehalaa 5 ||
jo eis maarae soee sooraa ||
jo eis maarae soee pooraa ||
jo eis maarae thisehi vaddiaaee ||
jo eis maarae this kaa dhukh jaaee ||1||
aisaa koe j dhubidhhaa maar gavaavai ||
eisehi maar raaj jog kamaavai ||1|| rehaao ||
Gauree, Fifth Mehla:
One who kills this is a spiritual hero.
One who kills this is perfect.
One who kills this obtains glorious greatness.
One who kills this is freed of suffering. ||1||
How rare is such a person, who kills and casts off duality.
Killing it, he attains Raja Yoga, the Yoga of Meditation. ||1||
Pause||

(Guru Arjun Dev 237)

The absence of Haumai, or separate sense of self is the experience of non-duality.It is the shift of awareness from Haumai to awareness itself that creates an encounter as Oneness, present moment, non-dual experience of Reality. The individuals function perfectly, harmoniously yet without the ego-centric separated sense of "me".

The Sikh sacred texts provide authentic sources and resources from self-realised researchers of consciousness on mind and existence which enable the transformation of self from Manmukh (ego facing) to Gurmukh (self-realised sovereign state).

ਮਨਮੁਖ ਮੈਲੇ ਮਲੁ ਭਰੇ ਹਉਮੈ ਤ੍ਰਿਸਨਾ ਵਿਕਾਰੁ ॥

Manamukh Mailae Mal Bharae Houmai thrisanaa Vikaar ||

Manmukhs (identified as Haumai) are polluted (conditioned), consumed with egotism, craving and distortion.

(Guru Amar Das Ang 29)

Gurmukh is when the shift of awareness is outside of the ego-centric mind or Haumai, and aware of awareness itself. This produces experiences of enlightenment, wisdom and Presence. Our human life provides us with this unique opportunity to set the stage for this shift.

Sehajae Aavai Sehajae Jaae ||
Man Thae Oupajai Man Maahi Samaae ||
Guramukh Mukatho Bandhh N Paae ||
With natural ease one comes, with natural ease one departs.
originating from mind, merging within the mind.
As Gurmukh, one is liberated and not bound.

(Raag Gauri Guru Nanak Dev Ang:152)

Sukh, Dukh and Anand - Pain, pleasure and Anand

Dukh and Sukh, suffering and absence of suffering are the basic experiences of ordinary consciousness in everyday life and dependent on the ego.

ਦੁਖਿ ਸੁਖਿ ਏਹੁ ਜੀਉ ਬਧੁ ਹੈ ਹਉਮੈ ਕਰਮ ਕਮਾਇ ॥

Dhukh sukh Eaehu Jeeo Badhh Hai houmai Karam Kamaae ll

Jeev (embodied consciousness) is bound in pleasure and pain, through the actions of its ego.

(Sri Raag: Guru Amar Das Ang 67)

Sukh is defined as pleasure, comfort and absence of discomfort, whereas dukh is unpleasant, uncomfortable, suffering, misery, unhappiness and physical pain.However, Gurmat offers a third possibility of Anand, or a state of non-dual, unified blissfulness, beyond both dukh and sukh.

ਦੁਖ ਸੁਖ ਗੁਰਮੁਖਿ ਸਮ ਕਰਿ ਜਾਣਾ ਹਰਖ ਸੋਗ ਤੇ ਬਿਰਕਤੁ ਭਇਆ ॥
ਆਪੁ ਮਾਰਿ ਗੁਰਮੁਖਿ ਹਰਿ ਪਾਏ ਨਾਨਕ ਸਹਜਿ ਸਮਾਇ ਲਇਆ ॥੧੨॥੭॥

Dhukh Sukh Guramukh Sam Kar Jaanaa Harakh Sog Thae Birakath Bhaeiaa ll

Aap Maar Guramukh Har Paaeae Naanak Sehaj Samaae Laeiaa ll12ll7ll

Gurmukh looks upon pain and pleasure as one and the same; he remains untouched by joy and sorrow.
Conquering self-conceit, the Gurmukh finds the One; O Nanak, intuitively merging within Existence.

(Raag Raamkali Guru Nanak Dev 907)

One way to understand what suffering means is to bring awareness and appreciation to the state of non-suffering (Sukh). Our lives are bound within the polarities of sukh (pleasure or comfort) and dukh (discomfort or suffering). Sukh may also be recognised as a state of flourishing which is the product of mental balance and transparent insight into the nature of reality. Dukh is therefore is a state of dis-harmony experienced as a "sense of unsatisfactoriness" and as suffering and pain arising from within one self.

Suffering is not only experienced as a result of the major events like death of a loved one, divorce or illness, but also experienced in day to day life. Suffering is being let down, anxiety, panic attacks, chronic stress, depression, conflicts withinourselves and with others. In other words, suffering is psychologically experienced as resistance to the way things are. Although suffering appears to be intimately linked with events in our daily lived life, being psychological in nature, it also provides us with an opportunity to learn how to break free of this internal suffering.

Pain or discomfort x resistance = suffering

To help us understand the psychological component of dukh, it is useful to differentiate physical pain from psychological distress and suffering. While pain cannot be avoided, it does not have to become suffering.

Pain can be divided into four layers, the ground layer being sensations, the second layer is the categorisation of the sensations experience into pleasant, unpleasant or neutral, the third layer is the judgement, whether we "like" or "dislike" the experience, and the final layer is the story supporting the judgement. Mindfulness in pain management targets the "story" layer which helps reduce the suffering and allow sensations to be experienced as sensations without suffering.

Suffering can be defined as the difference between what we crave and what is, the bigger we perceive this difference, the greater is our suffering. The cause of all suffering rests with our ego, or our false sense of self and its craving and bondage to its attachments.

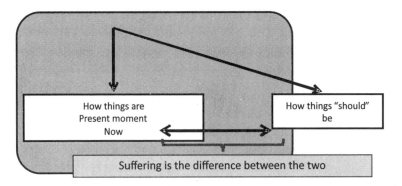

sireeraag mehalaa 3 ||

jag houmai mail dhukh paaeiaa mal laagee dhoojai
    bhaae ||

mal houmai dhhothee kivai n outharai jae so theerathh
    naae ||

bahu bidhh karam kamaavadhae dhoonee mal laagee
    aae ||

parriai mail n outharai pooshhahu giaaneeaa jaae ||1||

Siree Raag, Third Mehla:

*The world is polluted with the filth of egotism, suffering in
    pain. This filth sticks to them because of their love of
    duality.*

*This filth of egotism cannot be washed away, even by
    taking cleansing baths at hundreds of sacred shrines.*

*Performing all sorts of rituals, people are smeared with
    twice as much filth.*

*This filth is not removed by studying. Go ahead, and ask
    the wise ones. ||1||*

(Guru Amar Daas ji 39)

Suffering, unlike physical pain, can be defined as the
craving for circumstances to be different than they are, and
thus is psychological. While everyone desires happiness,
almost all of us pursue it in the wrong way. Our lives are
wasted in a never-ending struggle to satisfy our attachments
to what we think will make us happier while being ignorant

of the fact that the very things, objects, positions, we so desperately link with our perceived happiness, yet remain ignorant that they contain the seeds of suffering and unhappiness within.

> sukh ko maagai sabh ko dhukh n maagai koe ||
> *Everyone begs for happiness; no one asks for suffering.*
> sukhai ko dhukh agalaa manamukh boojh n hoe ||
> *But in the wake of happiness, there comes great suffering.*
> *The self-willed manmukhs do not understand this.*
> (Guru Nanak sggs 57)

For example, one may consider that money will bring happiness, and spend most of our adult life working tirelessly to accumulate it, while ignoring the impact of ongoing stress on their health, getting consumed by fear of losing our objects of attachment, or getting angry at not achieving our object of attachment. Prolonged stress, anger and fear all give rise to physiological changes in the body's biochemistry, blood pressure, heart rate in addition to the cocktail of hormones, proteins and anticoagulants to mention but a few. These, in turn create a toxic environment in the body which generate the conditions for cell malfunction, high levels of cell toxicity and lower immunity, giving rise to disease and illnesses.

This insatiable addictive behaviour inevitably generates unhealthy emotions, such as feelings of separation, fear, anger, jealously and depression. Lusting after our attachments gives rise to many other components which generate suffering. We become fearful of not achieving our attachments, feel anger at anyone or anything that stands in the way of our attachments, feel jealous of others who may have what we are attached to and finally become depressed as we lose hope.

Nanak dukheeaa sabhu sansaar:
O Nanak, the whole world is suffering Guru Nanak Dev ji.
(SGGS 954)

The seeds of our suffering or dukh is "Icha" or craving (trisanaa). The changing nature of sufferings can be seen throughout our lives, where a child experiences less suffering than someone in their youth, who is turn experience less suffering than an adult. Craving is the roots of ego bondage.

ਦੂਖਿ ਸੁਖਿ ਏਹੁ ਜੀਉ ਬਧੁ ਹੈ ਹਉਮੈ ਕਰਮ ਕਮਾਇ ॥

Dhukh Sukh Eaehu Jeeo Badhh Hai Houmai Karam Kamaae II
Beings are bound by pleasure and pain, through deeds done in egotism.
(Sri Raag Guru Amar Das Ang:67)

Haumai is one side of the coin, with suffering being the other. There are three sub-divisions of suffering, "Thinay tap" (three fevers), namely, psychological, psycho-physiological and physiological suffering.

Each of the three sub-divisions of suffering is defined by the constituent from which they arise. The gunas are the qualities or modes of material nature and correspond to the trimorphic nature of reality, creation, sustenance and destruction. Passion or activity (rajas) creates, goodness or essence (sattva) sustains and ignorance or inertia (tamas) destroys. These three are ranked hierarchically, with ignorance considered the lowest and goodness the highest. These three Gunas in varying degrees are the foundation from which the phenomenal world is experienced.There are no equivalent terms in the English language for the Gunas. However, one may understand them as follows, Sattva, can be considered the essence (like wetness in water), Rajas as movement and activity (flow of energy) and Tamas as inertia (substance).

The Gunas are in a constant process of change and responsible for phenomena of nature. Past and present are due to the different modes of manifestation of these three Gunas. The whole manifested universe is a changing combination of the three Gunas, which in turn also reflect the state of mind.Qualities of Gunas include:

Sattva	Ragas	Tamos
Pleasure	Pain	Attachment - ignorance
Self-actualization level	Self-esteem level	Basic needs level
goodness (sattva) sustains	Passion (rajas) creates	ignorance (tamas) destroys
Illumination	Movement	Obstruction
Inactivity	Activity	Inactivity
Essence e.g (Wetness in water)	Flow-movement e.g (flow of water)	Inertia –substance e.g (substance of water)
contentment, serenity, poise, calmness, discrimination, transparency, compassion, altruism, dispassion	love of fame, passion, lust, strife, impatience, jealousy, pride, arrogance	anger, greed, ignorance, resistance, inertia, forgetfulness, confusion, cruelty
Adhi - psychological physiological	Vyadi – psycho-	Upadhi - physiological

"Adhi" is caused by the mind and experienced as purely psychological suffering. This type of suffering is experienced from processes like cravings or infatuation, and can be a malfunction of Sattvic Guna.

"Vyadhi"is suffering, both at a psychological level and at a gross physical level. This type of suffering is experienced in the mind also manifests in the body related to external objects and events. This type of suffering is experienced from processes, such as cravings or infatuation and can be a malfunction and dominance of Ragas Guna

"Upadhi" is caused and experienced predominantly as bodily suffering. This type of suffering is experienced from processes linked to genetics, inflammation or exposure and is a malfunction and dominance of Tamos Guna

According to Gurmat, it is not possible to liberate oneself from these three types of suffering without encountering anauthentic (Guru) or self-realised teacher.

Gurmat differentiates Guru from Satguru.Guru means a teacher (one who may have the knowledge) and Satguru means authentic teacher (one who has the experience or self-realised) someone who has themselves arrived internally at a place beyond pleasure and suffering, through disciplined practices of mindfulness, selflessness and exploring the nature or essence of reality.

ਤਨ ਮਹਿ ਹੋਤੀ ਕੋਟਿ ਉਪਾਧਿ ॥
ਉਲਟਿ ਭਈ ਸੁਖ ਸਹਜਿ ਸਮਾਧਿ ॥
ਆਪੁ ਪਛਾਨੈ ਆਪੈ ਆਪ ॥
ਰੋਗੁ ਨ ਬਿਆਪੈ ਤੀਨੋ ਤਾਪ ॥੨॥

Than Mehi Hothee Kott Oupaadhh ॥
Oulatt Bhee Sukh Sehaj Samaadhh ॥
Aap Pashhaanai Aapai Aap ॥
Rog N Biaapai Theena Thaap ॥2॥

My body was afflicted with millions of diseases.
They have been transformed into the peaceful, tranquil harmony of Oneness.
When one understands one self,
One no longer suffers from illness and the three fevers. ॥2॥

(Raag Gauri Bhagat Kabir Ang:327)

Theenae Thaap Nivaaranehaaraa Dhukh Hanthaa Sukh Raas ॥

Three fevers are removed by experiencing the un-conditioned mind, suffering is destroyed and peace abides.

(741 Guru Arjun Dev)

Gurmat recognises the link between psychology and physiology, that the mind is connected both with the body (physiology) and emotions. It is by addressing psychological health that one can influence the physical health through contemplative practices, selfless actions and comprehending the nature of reality.

Gurmat recognises that while one seeks pleasure one fails to realise the seeds of suffering are contained in the pleasure itself. To illustrate this point, one may seek happiness through the acquisition of object, or from a partner or child. However, the very things that bring us happiness will also bring us pain when they are damaged, or when our loved ones are ill, leave or die. The suffering can increase significantly when one does not realise the changing nature of reality, the temporary nature of existence, relationships, life and so on. Attachment to objects, individuals, pleasures and ideas will inevitably lead to psychological distress and anguish, as everything is in a constant flux of change, and has a limited life span

ਸੁਖ ਕਉ ਮਾਗੈ ਸਭੁ ਕੋ ਦੁਖੁ ਨ ਮਾਗੈ ਕੋਇ ॥
ਸੁਖੈ ਕਉ ਦੁਖੁ ਅਗਲਾ ਮਨਮੁਖਿ ਬੂਝ ਨ ਹੋਇ ॥
ਸੁਖ ਦੁਖ ਸਮ ਕਰਿ ਜਾਣੀਅਹਿ ਸਬਦਿ ਭੇਦਿ ਸੁਖੁ ਹੋਇ ॥੫॥

Sukh Ko Maagai Sabh Ko Dhukh N Maagai Koe ॥
Sukhai Ko Dhukh Agalaa Manamukh Boojh N Hoe ॥
Sukh Dhukh Sam Kar Jaaneeahi Sabadh Bhaedh Sukh Hoe ॥5॥

Everyone begs for pleasure; no one asks for suffering.
But in the wake of pleasure, there is suffering. The man-
  mukhs (identified with the ego) do not understand this.
Those who see pain and pleasure as one and the same
  find peace; they are pierced through by the Shabad. ॥5॥
                    (Sri Raag Guru Nanak Dev Ang:57)

Mistaking pleasure to be "real" and assuming it to be

constant or unchanging, the Haumai attaches itself to that which is transitory. This attachment becomes the cause of suffering. Both pleasure and suffering are transitory in nature, like dreams, only appearing real, or permanent.

ਰੰਗ ਰਸਾ ਜੈਸੇ ਸੁਪਨਾਹਾ ॥

Rang Rasaa Jaisae Supanaahaa ॥

Enjoyments and pleasures are like just a dream.

(Raag Asa Guru Arjan Dev Ang:392)

Suffering, the medicine

While everyone wants to avoid suffering, suffering itself is the medicine which awakens and motivates oneself to act. The cause of suffering results from haumai, and its sense of preservation. Seeking permanency and fulfilment, haumai, our false sense of self develops attachments (Moh) with objects, beliefs, thoughts, emotions, body, desires and so on. Physical or psychological separation from the objects of attachments gives rise to suffering, which become the medicineto the disease of our attachments.

ਦੁਖੁ ਦਾਰੂ ਸੁਖੁ ਰੋਗੁ ਭਇਆ ਜਾ ਸੁਖੁ ਤਾਮਿ ਨ ਹੋਈ ॥

Dhukh Dhaaroo Sukh Rog Bhaeiaa Jaa Sukh Thaam N Hoee ॥

Suffering becomes the medicine, when pleasure is the disease, and does not remain pleasure.

(Raag Asa: Guru Nanak Dev Ang 469)

How does attachment become the disease?

Whatever the haumai attaches itself to, it identifies itself through its attachments and with its attachments. To maintain, preserve or defend these attachments, the haumai triggers the body's threat response system, which in turn changes its biochemistry and a host of other physical changes such as blood pressure, blood flow, heart rate, and sweating and

body temperature. The continuous maintenance of attachments is a form of psychological self-preservation, which
inevitably manifests as stress, anxiety, fear, anger and
disappointment, all of which create an unhealthy psychological
and physiology state.

ਹਰਿ ਜਪਿ ਜਪਿ ਅਉਖਧ ਖਾਧਿਆ
ਸਭਿ ਰੋਗ ਗਵਾਤੇ ਦੁਖਾ ਘਾਣਿ ॥੨॥

Har Jap Jap Aoukhadhh Khaadhhiaa Sabh Rog Gavaathae
Dhukhaa Ghaan || 2||

*I take the medicine of meditation on Naam, which has
cured all diseases and multitudes of sufferings.*
(Ang 651 Line 7 Raag Sorath: Guru Amar Das)

ਗੁਰਿ ਮੰਤੁ ਅਵਖਧੁ ਨਾਮੁ ਦੀਨਾ ਜਨ ਨਾਨਕ ਸੰਕਟ ਜੋਨਿ ਨ ਪਾਇ ॥੫॥੨॥

Gur Manthra Avakhadhh Naam Dheenaa Jan Naanak
Sankatt Jon N Paae ||5||2||

*One who is blessed with the medicine of the GurMantra,
O servant Nanak, does not suffer the agonies of
reincarnation.*
(3. Ang 1002 Line 1 Raag Maaroo: Guru Arjan Dev)

Psychophysiology – How psychological states impacts our body and our physiology

Gurmat clearly recognises that the mind and body are
connected, and one's psychological states generate both
emotions and impact the physiology of the body.

Suffering can be described as an event which creates
a stress response, it can be a stimulus or threat that causes
stress, for example. being late, feeling isolated, events
likeexams, divorce, death of loved one, moving house, being
diagnosed with a disease. For our purpose, stressors can
be divided into two categories, physical stressors and
psychological stressors. Physical stressor can be life events
or environmental circumstances, such as, extreme heat,

cold, lack of food or water, whereas psychological stress can be defined as a "reaction to a perceived demand or threat".

Psychological "threats" (suffering or dukh) can be created as a mental state by unconsciously identifying with stories we keep telling ourself about ourself. For example, you may have a stomach ache and begin to "imagine" (telling yourself stories) that this is the symptom of a serious illness, what is likely to happen to you as a result this illness, what will happen to your quality of life, who will look after you, so on and so forth. Before long you will begin to experience emotions such as fear and anxiety, which will also manifest as physical sensations in your body, like a pounding heart beat, excessive sweating, dry throat, butterflies in the stomach and so on.

When we are stressed (feel threatened), we triggers biochemical and physiological changes in our bodies, which include:

Pupils dilate

Increase in sweat production

Dry mouth and reduced salivary actions increased respiration and breathing

Increase in blood clotting

Increase in hormones including adrenaline and cortisol

Slower digestion

Decrese in urine production

Increase in blood pressure

Faster heart rate

Tighteness and tensing of muscles

Bowel and Bladder sphincter close

Increased central nervous system (CNS) activity and mental activity

Increased output of blood cholesterol

These biological changes are necessary for the body in order to take appropriate actions to eliminate the threat. This process can be divided into three phases, alarm, reaction/resistance and exhaustion.

1. Alarm phase, when the body automatically organizes physiological responses to fight-flight-freeze responses to threat.
2. Reaction and Resistance phase, which enables the body to continue its response, stabilizing the body's adaptations to stress.
3. The Exhaustion phase, when the body has depleted its reserves and can no longer maintain responses to the stressors.

After about 20 mins or so, the body restores itself into its homeostatic balance again. However, ongoing chronic or unresolved stress does not allow the body to restore its internal balance, impacting the immune system which is normally there to fight off infections and promote healing. The seriousness of chronic stress can not be under-estimated and has been shown to be a major contribuitor to illnesses and diseases ranging from frequent colds or flu, infections, slow wound healing to cancer or tumor development, depression, increased allergic responses, auto-immune diseases (rheumatoid arthritis, lupus, and scleroderma).[27,28,29,30]

Emotions

Gurmat considers emotions not to be a separate concept, but an energetic component that arises from contact with ego-complex haumai or ahamkara with the external stimuli through the five senses and interpreted by the various components of the mind. Emotions are modification of desire and attachment.

Emotions are seen from the context of haumai (ego complex) and atma, embodied consciousness's, they arise from desire and motivate action and are bi polar in nature, divided broadly as suffering or non-suffering. Suffering implied emotions giving rise to unhealthy physiological conditions. Emotions are all important and powerful feedback mechanism, which with awareness can be used to respond to stimuli without compromising health.

The cause of desire is the sense of imperfection, deficiency and non-fulfilment felt within the ego-self or haumai. Motivated by the temporary experience of gratification (Sukh), the ego-complex gives rise to more desires (greed or lobh), unfulfilled desires give rise to Karodh (anger),dukh (suffering) and unsatisfactory sense of imperfection or deficiency. The fulfilment of desires also strengthens the haumai or egos arrogance, or "Ahamkara", I-am-ness. Additionally, fear is experienced of losing what may possess or the fear of not attaining the object of desire.

These emotional states distort one's intellectual discrimination or "Buddhi", as ones awareness is automatically fused with the content of the mind, both thoughts and emotions. The desire and attachment create a false sense of self, and these ego-attachments, attractions and aversion become the mental afflictions or "Klesha".

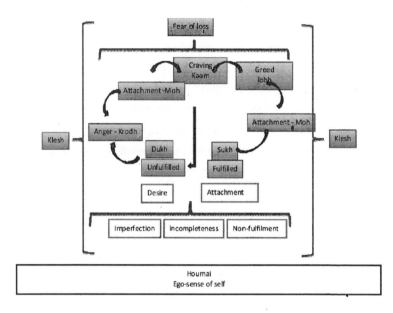

Psychophysiology : Flight-freeze-fight

Human beings have an inbuilt system known as a threat response system. Its primary function is to preserve our life, it enables us to detect threats that give rise to emotions like anxiety, anger, fear or disgust which in turn motivate us to act. Experiencing these emotions in turn prompt us to take appropriate actions to protect, eliminate or remove ourselves from the threatening situation. The emotions, like pain are the feedback mechanism reflecting our interaction with external stimuli, or internal perceived threats.

The emotion of fear may prompt us to run away. This is known as the flight response, whereas a burst of anger may motivate to fight. In circumstances in which we may be overwhelmed with emotions like fear which may shock to being incapable to movement, the freeze response.

Whilst the experience of such emotions may be difficult and even painful, their evolutionary function is primarily to protect us and they form part of our biological and psychological makeup. Our brains are wired to override pleasant sensations and give priority to addressing threats, making it easy to experience and trigger response. Our basic threat system is an automatic and instantaneous response system which does not allow time to think, it simply reacts because it operates on the principle of "better safe than sorry".[31],[32],

Gurmat asserts there are five natural tendencies within human beings which are all triggers to the flight-fight-freeze response system. These five are termed as "panj chor", the five thieves as they steal one away from the Present moment awareness and embroil the haumai into conditioned patterns of behaviour and reactions.[34]

The five are specific mental and emotional qualities which when uncontrolled and unrestricted are destructive both to oneself and to others too. These are **Ahankar** (I-am-maker), **Moh** (attachment), **Lobh** (greed), **Koardh** (anger) and **Kam** (craving or lust), also known as the 5 "Vikaars" or defects.

ਪੰਚ ਚੋਰ ਚੰਚਲ ਚਿਤੁ ਚਾਲਹਿ ॥
ਪਰ ਘਰ ਜੋਹਹਿ ਘਰੁ ਨਹੀ ਭਾਲਹਿ ॥
ਕਾਇਆ ਨਗਰੁ ਢਹੈ ਢਹਿ ਢੇਰੀ ਬਿਨੁ ਸਬਦੈ ਪਤਿ ਜਾਈ ਹੇ ॥੩॥

Panch Chor Chanchal Chith Chaalehi ||
Par Ghar Johehi Ghar Nehee Bhaalehi ||
Kaaeiaa Nagar Dtehai Dtehi Dtaeree Bin Sabadhai Path
Jaaee Hae ||3||

The five thieves cause the fickle consciousness to waver.
It considers the homes of others, but does not search its
own home.
The body-village crumbles into dust; without the Word of
the Shabad, one's honor is lost. ||3||

(Guru Nanak 1021)

These five qualities inevitably lead to suffering and

break an individual from beingaware (Gurmukh) to identifying automatically with the content of their minds and emotions (Manmukh) and being led or conditioned because of this "hijacking". To illustrate how the "Vikaars" influence and operate, consider the following:

When we feel threatened or angry, we experience "unpleasantness" and "discomfort", which motivates us to act to change,reduce or remove these sensations. Anger is normally expressed as an outburst of energy and would be useful in circumstances that required one to preserve oneself when under threat or attack. Anger also arises when our desires are unmet, prevented or threatened in any way or when our ego-complex is threatened for example by insults.

For example, you are walking at night alone and suddenly you hear a crash and someone leaps in front of you.Instantly you experience emotions and sensations which prompt an automatic reaction of running away, taking a stand and confronting the threat or simply freezing. In this instance the threat is very real and physical.

Once again we can use the same example, you are walking at night alone and hear some noise behind you.Immediately your senses are heightened, you begin to imagine someone is following you. Your thoughts are now creating a "story" in which it will present the possibilities of what this noise could be, recall any information or stories you have heard which re-create a similar scenario, consider of all the possible things that may happen to you, and before you know it, you begin to experience fear, anxiety; you can hear your heart beat, your palms begin to sweat, your behavior changes as you increase your steps. This is a psychological threat, in which you donot face a real threat, yet create a mental state which triggers the emotions of fear, anger or anxiety.[35]

Since our brain is pre-programmed to protect and preserve life, we are highly sensitive to dangers and threats of any kind and frequently overestimate dangers or perceived threats. Whilst we can be easily triggered into these highly aroused and alert states, it is far more difficult and takes significantly longer to restore emotional balance, unless of course we train ourselves to do so! However, before we explore how we can easily learn to de-activate effects of an activated threat system, say when we experience being stressed, anxious, angry most of the time, we need to learn a little more about how we function.[36]

Emotions like anxiety, fear, anger, aggression and stress although inevitable and useful in times of genuine threatening situations.However, when prolonged, these negative emotions trigger a wide range of health and social problems for individuals. For those diagnosed with diabetes, cancer, hypertension or CVD these negative emotions can have a significantly detrimental impact on your health, worsening existing conditions but also giving rise to additional medical complications. "Negative" emotions imply those sustained emotional states that lead to unhealthy physiological conditions and not imply one emotion is better than another, since all emotions are part of a feedback mechanism.[36]

For example, fear and anxiety together with acute and chronic stress impact immune system function and lead to stress related health disorders. Anger and its poor management are linked to heart disease and some types of cancers. Anger and resentment has been found to delay wound healing.

Our instinctive response to threats and danger give rise to the threat-stress-response, flight, fight or freeze. However, when we generate psychological threat based mental and emotional states then flight becomes self-isolation, fight become self-criticism and freeze becomes self-absorption or getting absorbed in our thoughts which in turn perpetuate the threat-stress-response, generating more negative emotions and worsening our internal physiological environment, increasing toxicity and chances for cell malfunction.[33,34]

Relaxation (soothing and contentment) response system – cultivating wholesome emotions

Just as we have a threat response system, which, when activated, generates negative emotions that force us to act, our bodies are also programmed with a relaxation (soothing and contentment) response system which helps generate positive emotions like contentment, kindness, affection, joy and calmness. Unlike negative emotions, such as anger, fear, anxiety and stress, positive emotions do not motivate us towards specific actions in the same way.Instead, positive emotions spark mental or cognitive changes, helping the body to restore its internal balance and neutralize the detrimental impact of negative emotions, giving rise to a sense of well-being and health. Negative emotions narrow the range of thought and actions, demanding quick and focused response to any life-threatening situation whereas positive emotions broaden and help build and strengthen our personal health resources', such as, improving immune system function, reducing blood pressure, increasing brain dopamine levels (feel good hormones).[37]

The activation of this system enables us to experience a sense of calmness, contentedness and peacefulness which, in turn, changes our biochemistry and physiology in the following ways to mention a few:

These include:

Decreased blood pressure

Decreased sweat production
Slower respiration, breathing and metabolic rate
Quicker wound healing
Decrease in stress hormones like adrenaline or cortisol
Restore balance of digestive system
Decreases heart rate
Relaxed muscles
Decreased mental activity
Decreased output of blood cholesterol
Release of endorphins

Just like animals, when we do not have an internal striving or drive to achieve or do anything, recognizing that we have sufficiently enough to meet our needs, we experience contentment, feelings of being safe and internal peacefulness.

People who practice meditation as a consistent part in their life experience arrive at these feelings of contentment, calm, safety and peace by de-activating the threat response system. Contentment is a form of happiness, coupled with feelings of safety and acceptance of things being the way they are.

The soothing and contentment system is our inbuilt nurturing system.For example, when a child is distressed, parents respond with affection and care to calm and soothe the child. Affection, kindness and soothing from others help us to feel safe, which in turn helps release powerful chemicals in our brains called endorphins which are associated with feelings of wellbeing, contentment and peace.

Contentment or peace is not something that is outside yourself, but something within us. Our modern lifestyle is more likely to condition us towards activating the threat response system through work demand, financial demands, continuous and constant life or life style threatening "news" being pushed at us in every walk of life. This constant threat-stress-based lifestyle maintains many of us in mental states of anxiety, fear and anger. If we were being diagnosed with a terminal illness such as diabetes or cancer, we also generate unhealthy emotions like anxiety, anger, fear and stress, which, in turn, add to and increase demands on our self to escape or remove this threat maintain unhealthy physiological conditions like high blood pressure, high glucose levels, high levels of stress hormones and impaired kidney function.[38]

How we create our own suffering

Once we understand how our body responds to stresses and threats, we can appreciate how these changes in our physiology and biochemistry can infact worsen any existing disease adding to complications as well as giving rise to new diseases and illnesses because of chronic stress. Ongoing stress has a detrimental impact on the body's' biochemistry and the immune system. Research shows that stress contributes to the development of major illnesses, like as heart disease, cancers, depression and obesity.[39]

Every thought generates its corresponding emotions and sensations in our body, as the mind and body are interconnected and form a continuum.Happy thoughts give rise to positive emotions, whilst negative thoughts give rise to negative emotions and tightness in specific parts of the body.

For example, worrisome thoughts about your future or guilt about your past actions will generate negative emotions (unhealthy states), like fear and anxiety, in the same way as you being threatened by a predator. Triggering a flood of stress related hormones like Cortisol, which affects your immune system, heart rate, blood pressure,effecting, every single cell in your body. Unfortunately, most people have such thoughts hundreds or even thousands of times a day, not recognising their impact, and therefore injecting fear, anger, aggression, resentment, guilt and anxiety, especially those who suffer from illnesses.

In modern society and, particularly, in the Western world, the effects of thinking on our body has only recently been recognized. Humans have the unique ability to create unhealthy mental states which impact health and wellbeing. There is no training of any kind offered in the schooling system which help individuals learn the harmful effects of certain types of thinking, how to dis-identify from the continuous thought streams or how to cultivate healthy and wholesome mental states. Unfortunately, such ignorance has manifested itself in the overwhelming presence of diseases like diabetes, coronary heart conditions, depression and cancers.[39] This lack of awareness is perhaps the greatest cause of human suffering in the modern world.Thoughts divide us within ourselves and others and are the greatest source of human misery.

We spend almost all our time occupied, thinking either of the past, or fantasies about the future, yet miss out the only place we really are, here and in the moment of now.

We believe what we think to be true; our thoughts are never challenged by ourselves.We continue to identify ourselves with our thoughts and the emotions they generate. This identification is known as cognitive fusion, an involuntary and unconscious process. Imagine your thoughts to be like a pair of sunglasses which you forget you are wearing and, therefore, you are unaware that your perceptions are being coloured by them. Cognitive fusion combined with avoiding difficult emotions tend to pull us out of the present moment and into "stories" we keep telling ourselves and believing our thoughts to be "true or facts". These thoughts become especially harmful when they are self-critical, self-isolating leading us towards self-absorption.

Self-critical thinking will give rise to emotions like anger and aggression, while self-isolating thoughts give rise to fear, helplessness and hopelessness and self-absorbing thoughts lead to rumination and eventually depression.

Ego-complex conditioned behaviour and health

Haumai, or the ego-complex feels incomplete and thus needs to reassert itself at every opportunity, and seeks a sense of security or permanency. The need for permanency and self-assertion, is fuelled by trisanaa (craving or desire). Desire is an inherent quality within existence, and the catalyst for its unfolding, growth and evolution. However, it is not just desire which can impact health, but more importantly our attachment (Moh) to the objects of desire. In Gurmat, there are five psychological states which do not just take the individual out of the present moment, but also change the physiology within the body.

The cycle and process of this "loss of self" begins paradoxically with a need for securing the self, and overcoming the innate insecurity experienced by the ego-complex or Haumai. The haumai actively seeks attachments to make it feel secure and thus attaches itself emotionally with its objects of desire.

The five "thieves" increasingly fuse awareness with the content of the mind and other phenomena , removing our "presence" from here and now, and identify it with the objects of our attachment.

The identification process of the ego-complex with its object of attachment and consequential process takes place in several stages. However, the whole process is automatic and extremely fast. It first begins with the stimuli to the sensory organs, from which the "Chitta" (memory within the specific emotional climate) identifies and correlates it with memory. This is followed by judgement as attraction, aversion or indifference. This triggers the intention, followed by attention towards or away from the catalysing stimuli.

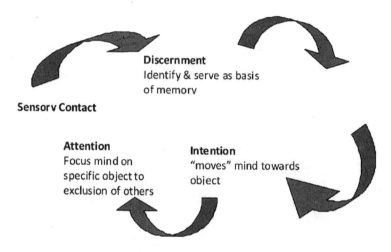

Discernment
Identify & serve as basis
of memory

Sensory Contact

Attention
Focus mind on
specific object to
exclusion of others

Intention
"moves" mind towards
object

The sense of attachment (moh) gives rise to yet other psychological patterns which increase towards a sense of craving/ grasping/ desiring (Trisha), again conditioning the mind towards greed (lobh), insatiable craving. Unfulfilled greed manifests as anger (karodh) and residual unresolved anger gives rise to yet more craving- or lust (Kaam) for another object of attachment, to begin the cycle again once again, Ahamkara or a continuous re-creation of the sense of "I" am-creator". This self-identification complex or the activity of ego is what is transcended with meditation practice of Naam Symran by drawing awareness to the Shabad or sound and gradually breaking free from the false sense of self, to directly experience pure consciousness or authentic self.

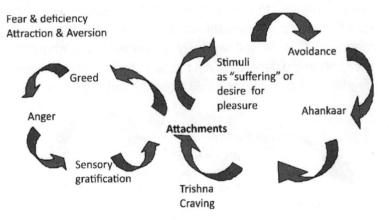

Eis Dhaehee Andhar Panch Chor Vasehi Kaam Krodhh
Lobh Mohu Ahankaaraa ll
Within this body dwell the five thieves: sensual craving, anger, greed, emotional attachment and I-am-ness.
(Guru Amar Das 600)

CHAPTER FOUR

Introducing Practises

Symran – Cultivation of mindful awareness

Symran and Naam Symran are the foundational practices in Gurmat, and are essential to meet two objectives. The first objective is to enable the body's' own self-regulating health system to restore the physiological homeostasis by cultivating awareness through attention training, and the second objective is through continued awareness cultivation to establish the bedrock for ego-transcendence and meet the ultimate objective of knowing oneself.

The word "Symran" comes from the Sanskrit word, "Smriti" or "Sati" in Pali, and it is found in Indictraditions that have been practicing, researching and documenting the model of the mind, cultivating awareness and self-inquiry for several thousand years. Symran is synonymous with the word Dhyana, which simply means awareness. Awareness can only be known by being aware.

Mindfulness is defined as paying attention purposefully to our moment by moment experience, with an accepting and non-judgmental attitude.Meditation can only be known by practicing it. For example, if you are hungry no-one else can eat for you or will listening to descriptions of food nourish you, only by consuming food yourself can you be nourished, and the same applies to meditation. Only by practicing mindfulness can we know meditation, more importantly, reap its remarkable healing benefits amongst other benefits.

Most people operate on "automatic pilot", state of mindlessness or manmukh, when our unawareness dominates our mind, almost half awake not available to the moment to moment life experience. You may "see" this for yourself when you get drive or even get into a shower. Even when we deliberately try to focus on one thing, we quickly discover how slippery it is to hold our awareness.

Our thoughts and emotions easily overwhelm our awareness, clouding our awareness of the present. Our awareness is hijacked and drawn by our sense organs, which include, sight, sound, feeling, taste or smell, all of which provide stimuli that capture attention and leads it very quickly into varying stages of consciousness. During this period, whatever its duration, we are lost in our thoughts and unaware of our actual experience.

ਮਨ ਅੰਤਰਿ ਹਉਮੈ ਰੋਗੁ ਭ੍ਰਮਿ ਭੂਲੇ ਹਉਮੈ ਸਾਕਤ ਦੁਰਜਨਾ ॥

Man Anthar Houmai Rog Bhram Bhoolae Houmai Saakath Dhurajanaa ||

Within the minds of the unaware is the disease of egotism, wander around lost, deluded by doubt.

(Salok Vaaraan and Vadheek: Guru Ram Das Ang 1424)

We spend most of our time thinking about the future or replaying some aspect from our past. Meditation is not about trying to feeling anything special or getting "somewhere". In fact, it is allowing yourself to be where you are, openly experiencing each moment by moment unfolding.

Symran or being present is not a technique but a way of being. Acceptance of ourselves exactly as we find our self at that present moment is a cornerstone of cultivating this way of being. It is about allowing yourself to be exactly where you are and as you are, and for the world to be exactly as it is in this moment as well. It is an act of compassion, kindness and love that recognizes our perfection even in our obvious imperfection. Awareness itself is the teacher, the student, and the lesson.

Learning to undo the effects of negative emotion

Our education systems are namely geared towards learning facts about everything, ranging from Astronomy to Quantum physics.Yet there is no education which enables us to learn about being aware. We,are therefore not taught to recognize and question the reality created by our continuous stream of thoughts, most of which are highly influenced by the constant propaganda of "bad news" bombarded with 24/7. Is it any wonder that diseases like depression, cancer, coronary heart disease and diabetes are increasing at such unprecedented levels?

We begin by first understanding the difference between the mind and awareness. The mind is our thinking, our intelligence, our memory and our sense of I-amness. Thoughts and memories give rise to corresponding emotions and bodily sensations.

Practice

Find a quiet place to sit for a few minutes, when ready close your eyes and "draw" a circle in your "minds'-eye" and hold your focus on this image for the next minute.

Were you able to first draw the circle? What colour was it? Were you able to hold your focus on the image? Did the image change at any time? Did it blur? Was your focus distracted by a thought or sensation or a sound?

Did you notice anything else? Did you notice that you were aware of the circle for whatever time, until your awareness was distracted or you stopped this exercise? Awareness is something apart from and different from all that which we are aware of. Our thoughts, emotions, images, sensations, desires and memory are the content we are aware off. Awareness is directed or focused consciousness. While awareness itself does not change, the content which we are aware of changes. Unfortunately, we do not know how to cultivate awareness and how to dis-identify from unhealthy our thoughts and emotions.

Just as we would learn not to swim in a choppy sea but in a calm and safe environment, we should learn to train our awareness by creating an appropriate environment in which you are unlikely to be disturbed for the duration of our practice which can range from 5 mins to 40 minutes. It is best to start with manageable time periods of a few minutes and then gradually build upon it. Like every other skill, we wish to learn, practice is essential, as is attitude. An attitude of openness and acceptance greatly benefits the process.

Awareness can be thought of as a zoom lens on a camera, by bringing our focus to any object we can zoom into that object with our attention and become aware of the object. This becomes particularly important when we consider how our thoughts, and the way we picture them in our minds, give rise to corresponding emotions. Where we place our focus, and zoom in will affect our emotions and body states.

Guun – Positive psychological states

Western or modern psychology has exclusively focused on pathology over its past 100 years of history, attempting to understand psychopathological "illnesses" like depression, anxiety, hysteria, obsessions, psychoses, compulsions, anger, panic attacks, personality disorders and so on, with little or no scientific research or theoretical thought to the value, cultivation, understanding or recognition of the profound health and wellbeing benefits of positive emotions such as compassion, gratitude, optimism and contentment.[40]

There has been increasing interest in the role of positive emotions of health and wellbeing. Positive emotions such as contentment, compassion, love and optimism are directly linked with increase in immunity, increase self-esteem, reduce impact of negative emotions, increase wound healing time reduce, alleviate or eliminate stress, anxiety and depression.[41]

In fact, Western medicine has now labelled virtually every human experience that is unpleasant as a "mental disorder" per the DSM V, (Diagnostic and Statistical Manual of Mental Disorders, Fifth Edition)the bible for "mental disorders". What is even more shocking is that the "disorders" listed in its 900 plus pages have no scientific evidence but are based on a votingsystem by a select group of mental health "professionals". Diagnosis of mental orders by these health professionals is based on subjectivity, and not any medical of scientific tests. Once diagnosed, one is placed on prescriptions of highly dubious and toxic antipsychotics. Currently, antipsychotic drugs are the third biggest cause of death after cancer and CVD.[41,42]

There are no objective tests in psychiatry, no X-ray, laboratory, or exam finding that says definitively that someone does or does not have a mental disorder."

(Allen Frances, Former DSM-IV Task Force Chairman)

"DSM-IV is the fabrication upon which psychiatry seeks acceptance by medicine in general. Insiders know it is more a political than scientific document...DSM-IV has become a bible and a money-making bestseller—its major failings notwithstanding."

(Loren Mosher, M.D., Clinical Professor of Psychiatry)

Gurmat psychotherapy focuses on the cultivation of positive or healthy emotional states, known as "Guun", and distinguishes it from "Augunn", unhealthy psycho-emotional states.

Research studies show negative emotions tend to narrow the individuals' thought-action repertoires urging specific action tendencies (e.g. attacks, fleeing or freezing), whereas positive emotions tend to broaden individuals' thought-action repertoires, prompting thoughts and actions typically, enjoyable, stress less and engaging (e.g. playing, exploring, engaging). Negative or unhealthy emotions require substantial energy (for example from attacks or when fleeing) and produce heightened cardiovascular reactivity that redistributes blood flow to relevant skeletal muscles, reduce immunity, change blood bio-chemistry and circulation.[43,44,45]

While the research is still in its infancy on the impact of cultivating positive emotions on health, research that is available in positive psychology has demonstrated the profound health impact of cultivating positive emotions. Increasing evidence suggests that meditation practices impact physiological pathways, including the immune and neuroendocrine system.[46]

The practice of Symran and especially Naam Symran, gives rise to the experience of contentment, which, over time and practice flourishes into self-compassion and compassion. Compassion, leads to the development of personal ethics and values, in addition to the recognition of the boundless gifts of personal life, engendering humility and gratitude.[47]

ਸਤੁ ਸੰਤੋਖੁ ਦਇਆ ਕਮਾਵੈ ਏਹ ਕਰਣੀ ਸਾਰ ॥

Sath Santhokh Dhaeiaa Kamaavai Eaeh Karanee Saar ॥

Practice truth (authenticity), contentment and compassion is the most excellent way of life.

(Sri Raag Guru Arjan Dev Ang:51)

bilaaval mehalaa 5 ॥

gobi(n)dh gobi(n)dh gobi(n)dh mee ॥

jab thae bhaettae saadhh dhaeiaaraa thab thae dhuramath dhoor bhee ॥1॥ rehaao ॥

pooran poor rehiou sa(n)pooran seethal saa(n)th dhaeiaal dhee ॥

kaam krodhh thrisanaa aha(n)kaaraa than thae hoeae sagal khee ॥1॥

sath sa(n)thokh dhaeiaa dhharam such sa(n)than thae eihu ma(n)th lee ॥

kahu naanak jin manahu pashhaaniaa thin ko sagalee sojh pee ॥2॥4॥90॥

Bilaaval, Fifth Mehla:

Chanting Gobind, Gobind, Gobind (Shabad), we become like Gobind.

Since I met the compassionate, Holy Saints, my ego-mindedness has been driven far away. ॥1॥Pause॥

The Perfect Oneness is perfectly pervading everywhere, cool, calm, peaceful and compassionate.

Sexual cravings, anger and egotistical desires have all been eliminated from my body. ॥1॥

Authenticity (truth), contentment, compassion, ethics and purity - I have received these from the Teachings of the Saints.

Says Nanak, one who realizes this in his mind, achieves total understanding. ॥2॥4॥90॥

Positive emotion	Impact on health
Compassion Self compassion	Increased self esteem Increase immunity Reduced cortisol responses Reduce impact of perceived stress, Eliminate burnout, Prevent depression and anxiety increases in life satisfaction[48]
Contentment	Stablise blood pressure Reduce anxiety Reduce cortisol [49,50]
Gratitude	Reduces inflammation Increases wound healing Increase retention of affective speech in adults with autism Increase trust & satisfaction Reduces fear & anxiety contributes to intimacy in relationships[51,52]
Optimism	Greater survival in cancer patients, slow menopause[53,54,55]
Authenticity	Optimum mental health, homestatis[56,57,58]

Positive emotions create an openness and transparency which helps develop constructive engagement with oneself and others thus developing healthy relationships all of which result in a sense of well being, meaning, purpose and achievement.[59,60,61]

Introduction to awareness training – right-mindfulness

Mindfulness is differentiated from correct or right-

mindfulness, samma sati or symran. Correct or right mindfulness is the practice of mindfulness with an understanding of
the approporiate worldview which refects the nature of reality
including our own self. If mindfulness practice is learning to
walk, then Gurmat provides the direction.

This simple exercise will introduce two aspects to you
Firstly, that you have awareness and secondly, that you have
the ability and control to move the focus of your attention and
cultivate awareness.

Before beginning the exercise, take a moment to notice
how you are feeling right now. Is there anything in particular
that is dominating your thoughts, particular types of thoughts?
What emotions are prevalent?

Find a comfortable posture where your back, neck and
head are aligned, your shoulders are relaxed and the souls
of your feet are firmly on the floor and place your hands on
your laps, palms facing down.

Once you are comfortable and seated, take a deep
breath in, making sure that your belly expands on the breath
in and then hold your breath for a moment or two, and
release, allowing the breath to exhale, repeat this process
two more times. When ready, try this

- Bring your focus onto your left foot
- Notice the sensations at the bottom of your left
  foot
- Now bring your focus onto the heel of your left foot,
  then the ankle and gradually your entire foot
- Hold your attention for about 30 seconds or so
- Now switch your focus onto your right foot and repeat
  the process
- Again hold your attention for about 30 seconds
- Now bring your focus on to your left hand, see if you
  can become aware of the palm of your left hand

- Are there any sensations present there? How do they feel?
- Bring your awareness to your fingers, starting with the little finger first, gradually moving it to your ring finger, index finger and the fore finger
- Bringing your focus onto the whole hand
- Hold your attention for about 30 seconds or so at this point
- Now switch your focus onto your right hand and repeat the process
- Bring your focus onto your lips, see if you notice any sensations here
- Moving to your mouth and tongue
- Is your tongue firm or soft?
- Finally bring your focus on your breath
- Notice the movement of the air through your nostrils, and, then, the movement back out again
- Try and maintain focus on the movement of your breath for the next 10 breaths as best as you can

When you have finished this exercise, take time to notice how you are feeling.

Hopefully you noticed that you have the ability to direct your focus like a zoon lens on specific parts of your body, bringing them into your field of awareness and while you had one specific part of your body within your field of attention, the rest of the body became "out of focus". Similarly, our emotions have the power to easily capture our focus and attention, like the previous exercise we can either zoom in or out. Normally, we tend to zoom into our emotional content and identify with in.

The purpose of this exercise is to give us the understanding and tools to make a choice between being driven by your negative emotions and thoughts or being aware and cultivating positive healthy emotions. Unfortunately, most of us have spent most of our lives being driven by our thoughts and emotions without even being aware that we have the ability to question these thoughts not to mention the ability to dis-identify from them. These are our psychological patterns, habits and consequently manifesting into our behavior.

The objective of this exercise is for us to see that we have the ability and control to direct our attention and to begin to learn to notice where it is and what it is focused. This was our first introduction to mindfulness, being aware of your present moment by moment experience.

Mindfulness and Mindlessness

What is mindfulness? Mindfulness is being aware, bringing your focus to the Present moment, maintaining the unfolding of your present moment-by-moment in your field of awareness with an attitude of openness and non-judgement. Mindfulness can only be known through experience of mindfulness, all words and descriptions are merely pointing towards the experience but not the experience itself. Just as we discovered previously in this book, the experience of burning is not the same as knowledge about burning![62,63]

To know mindfulness, it is important to recognise mindlessness. Mindfulness is not something hard or strenuous, it is relatively simple. However, the problem we face is remembering to become mindful. We forget and it is easy to forget, as most of our lives we have never been taught how to become aware and have been encouraged to live our lives as mindless robots. Look back over the past day; can you recall moments of awareness? If you travelled to work or shops, can you recall what you passed, how you were feeling and what you going on around you? The answer is probably, not! The reason is because we have conditioned ourselves to function on automatic pilot. The reasons we operate as mindless robots is that we have been programmed and conditioned, the consequences of our conditioning also creates a distorted and unhealthy view of ourselves and life. This programming has been reinforced and is being reinforced through media, religions, society and schooling.

The good news is that despite being conditioned, we have the ability to re-condition ourselves into healthier and more aware modes of being; to step out of automatic pilot routines which may be functional, but unless we recognise them and step out, we may wake up one day to discover "where did my life go?"

Pavan Guru and Shabd Guru, Breath and Sound teachers and anchor in the Present moment

ਪਵਣੁ ਗੁਰੂ ਪਾਣੀ ਪਿਤਾ ਮਾਤਾ ਧਰਤਿ ਮਹਤੁ ॥

Pavan guroo Paanee Pithaa Maathaa Dhharath Mehath ॥

Air is the guru, Water is the Father, and Earth is the Great Mother of all.

(Salok: Guru Nanak Dev Ang 8)

ਸਬਦੁ ਗੁਰੂ ਸੁਰਤਿ ਧੁਨਿ ਚੇਲਾ ॥

Sabadh Guroo Surath Dhhun Chaelaa ॥

Shabad is the guru, awareness is the disciple.

(Raag Raamkali: Guru Nanak Dev Ang 943)

To begin mindfulness practice we choose an object to focus our attention upon, this can be a sound as in Symran and transcendental meditation, body or breath. The simplest method is to begin with our breath. Before we develop our practice of mindfulness with the breath, it is useful to recognise, understand and appreciate our breath and the process of breathing.

Uncovering our Breath

A story is told of a wise man asking his students, how long is one's life?Some said, 70 years, another 100 years, some more and some less.The wise man replies, life is as long as our breath

Breath is the root of our existence, our life itself. It flows tirelessly, unimpeded, without a single pause, oxygenating every single cell in our body and removing the waste products of respiration like carbon dioxide.

Our breath is not only the most important part of us, but will also the most intimate. For the first thing we do is to take a breath in, to inhale, and the last thing we'll ever do is to exhale, breathe out. The breath accompanies us the moment we are born and remains with us until our last moment. We are our breath, in other words; we are unable to live without breathing.We begin life with breath and end with breath. While the breath is essential for our life, most of us go through life without giving our breath any notice, unless of course we are choking, unable to breathe, or coughing.

Consider this, did you come first or your breath?

Relationship between breath and mind

Breath and breathing are taken for granted in our everyday lives, yet the breath is essential for our being alive, and our breathing while always on "automatic", is a unique bodily function which can continue without any deliberate effort. However, can also be conscious and "self directed".

Our breathing has a deep and profound connection with

our emotional and mental states. The rhythm, depth and flow of our breathing and its processes change automatically to reflect our state of mind and emotions. When we are angry we tend to over-breathe as the body needs oxygen to meet the demands of being under "threat", to be able to react by fight, fleeing and freezing, "huffing and puffing". When one experiences anger, the breathing changes, the breath become faster, and its rhythm quickens and becomes irregular, even frantic.[64]

To experience this connection between your breath, mind and emotions, try this simple exercise.

Before beginning the exercise, settle into a comfortable posture and take a few moments to notice how you are feeling and how calm or disruptive your mind is. Once ready, exhale as deeply as you can, bringing your belly in and retain this for a few seconds, do not inhale yet, ensuring that all the air is out. Then when you are ready, simply relax and allow the body to inhale, slowly, deeply as much as you can. Again, stop and pause for a few seconds holding your breath, and when ready, allow the breath to exhale, once the breath is completely out, pause and hold for a few seconds, and then allow the body to breathe again. Follow this process for a few minutes. As best as you can, exhale totally and inhale totally creating a rhythm. Exhale, pause, breathe in, pause, breathe out; Pause after exhaling completely, hold your breathe for a few seconds, then inhale extending your belly out to fill your body cavity with the vital breath, hold, pause, when ready, relax and breath out.

After about 3-5 minutes, notice how you are feeling. Notice how this simple process has created a new climate within you. It is not surprising that the breath has been used as an anchor to focus on in meditation for more than 2500 years. The breath is always with us, no matter where we are, what we are doing, the breath is intrinsically linked to our mental and emotional conditions, and by changing our breathing we can alter both our mind states and emotional content.

By focusing our awareness on breath, we create the perfect conditions to both cultivate our awareness of the Present moment, and, allow the breath to find its own natural rhythm and flow.

ਤਿਸਹਿ ਧਿਆਵਹੁ ਸਾਸਿ ਗਿਰਾਸਿ ॥

Thisehi Dhhiaavahu Saas Giraas ||

Meditate on Oneness with every breath and morsel of food.
(Raag Gauri Sukhmanee: Guru Arjan Dev Ang 280 Line 18)

ਸਿਮਰਹੁ ਸਿਮਰਹੁ ਸਾਸਿ ਸਾਸਿ ਮਤ ਬਿਲਮ ਕਰੇਹ ॥

Simarahu Simarahu Saas Saas Math Bilam Karaeh ||

Meditate, meditate in remembrance with each and every breath - do not delay!
(Raag Bilaaval: Guru Arjan Dev Ang 812 Line 14)

ਸਾਸਿ ਸਾਸਿ ਪ੍ਰਭੁ ਮਨਹਿ ਸਮਾਲੇ ॥

Saas Saas Prabh Manehi Samaalae ||

Breath by breath cultivate Presence awareness.
(Raag Gauri: Guru Arjan Dev Ang 191 Line 7)

Symran-Sound, listening, awareness-the doorway to self-discovery

Our mind is constantly moving, hopping from one thing to another, replaying past or fantasying about the future or thinking about "me" or "the other". Our thoughts jumping around like a wild erratic monkey enclosed in a room with windows! As a result of this constant movement from one thought, feeling or sensation to another, we spend most of our lives living in our heads, on automatic pilot, relentlessly bombarded with thoughts, fears, and beliefs all of which we believe to be true without question! What if there was a way to bring yourself to a place of peace within your mind so you can hear the wisdom of our heart? A place which gives us strength, resilience and balance needed for recovery and health. There is and it is called mindfulness or Symran, remembering to re-member.

Symran is the practice of learning to focus our attention purposefully and non-judgmentally the unfolding of the present moment, moment by moment. The simplest method to cultivate mindfulness is to paying attention and listen. We can listen to our breath, or listen to a specific word, such as the sacred mantra "so-ham" or "har" or "satnaam". When we practise mindfulness and bring our focus to the movement of our breath as it flows in and out of your nostrils, we will begin to witness our thoughts and feelings, as though we are watching an interesting movie, without any judgment of our experience as pleasant, unpleasant or neutral—but observing the nature of "reality", as is!. Through mindfulness we discover a connection with our inner self and dis-connection with the automatic process of identification with our thoughts, feelings and sensations. This connection, which is strengthened by practicing mindfulness, is the foundation for our journey to health, wholeness and wellbeing.

Mindfulness heals and rebalances us because much of our emotional and psychological suffering arises from "automatic" unconscious reactions and routines. For example, people, when they feel anxious may resort to smoking, or turn to alcohol to numb unpleasant emotions or lash out when feeling angry "automatically".

Mindfulness enables us to **"take control"**, to become mindful or aware of patterns of reaction and this will enable to choose our response rather than react

ਰਤਨੁ ਪਦਾਰਥੁ ਘਰ ਤੇ ਪਾਇਆ ॥

ਪੂਰੈ ਸਤਿਗੁਰਿ ਸਬਦੁ ਸੁਣਾਇਆ ॥

ਗੁਰ ਪਰਸਾਦਿ ਮਿਟਿਆ ਅੰਧਿਆਰਾ ਘਟਿ ਚਾਨਣੁ ਆਪੁ ਪਛਾਨਣਿਆ ॥੭॥

Rathan Padhaarathh Ghar Thae Paaeiaa ||

Poorai Sathigur Sabadh Sunaaeiaa ||

Gur Parasaadh Mittiaa Andhhiaaraa Ghatt Chaanan Aap
Pashhaananiaa ||7||

*The Priceless Jewel is found, in the home of one's own
being,*

*When one listens to the Shabad, the Word of the Perfect
True Guru.*

*By Guru's Grace, the darkness of spiritual ignorance is
dispelled; I have come to recognize the Divine Light
within my own heart. ||7||*

(Raag Maajh Guru Amar Das Ang:129)

Symran practice enables awareness to dis-identify
from its content and develop the cultivation of awareness per
se. The Symran practise begins with the intention to be
present by focusing attention on breath, thoughts, sensations,
and, finally rests on listening to the internalised sound of the
mantra repetition.

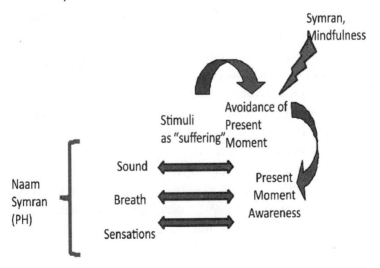

A simple mantra based meditation

Step 1: Begin by settling down in a quiet place
Bring your focus to the movement of your breath and simply observe the breath for a few minutes until the mind feels calm.

Step 2 *"Viakhari*: take a deep breath in and as you breathe out utter the mantra "So-hum" extending the "hum" so you can feel vibration in your mouth. Repeat this three times

Step 3 *"Madham":* Mutter "So ham" but this time without using the voice box, instead muttering the sound with the tongue only. Repeat this three times

Step 4 *"Pasanti"* : As you breathe in say "So" within your mind, and as you breathe out, say "hum" in your mind. Repeat this three times

Step 5 *"Para":* bring your awareness to your breath and begin to listen to the sound of your breath itself.

Approach to our practice - Attitude

Mindfulness effectively means "observing or witnessing". Bearing this in mind, and considering the discovery within Quantum Physics, that the very act of observation changes that which is observed.

The link between reality and observation is based on the 'Copenhagen Interpretation' of quantum mechanics proposed by Niels Bohr, Werner Heisenberg, and other physicists working in that city.

Similarly, in psychology, the observer effect or Hawthorne **effect**, refers to subjects altering their behaviour when they are aware that an **observer** is present. The act of observation changes the observed. In the practice of mindfulness, the act of self-observation in a non-judging and impartial manner enables the thoughts to "settle", such that one is able to cultivate "silence of mind, complimenting stillness of body and spaciousness of awareness".[65]

This has been recognised in most Eastern tradition many centuries ago through looking at the mind, discovering that the mind consists of events, and we participate in those events as we look inwards. What we are looking at responds to the process of looking, how we look at something determines what we see.

Attitude is perhaps one of the most important factors in facing any situation in life. An attitude of acceptance, non-resitatnce has a completely different impact on our physiology compared with an attitude of resistance and non-acceptance. Acceptance is to embrace whatever arises within us; emotions, feelings, thoughts and sensations, moment by moment, just as they are, without wishing to change them in any way.

Our attitude is vitally important with regards to the practice of mindfulness itself. Our attitude will determine what we gain from our mindfulness practice. To illustrate this, consider if one's approach is "I can't meditate, or mind was too busy for meditation or don't think this will do anything". When you then engage in your practice and discover that your mind is distracted from the breath far more than you'd expected or considered, these distractions are likely to confirm your suspicion, confirming the "truth" of your attitude. In other words, your attitude significantly alters what you get out of the practice. On the other hand, coming with an attitude of mindfulness being the panacea to all our ills, is also likely to disappoint. Therefore cultivating and maintaining particular kinds of attitude is an equally important component for the cultivation of mindfulness.

Our attitude is set by our intention, and we can begin

by distinguishing our intention to mindfulness in the following three ways.

1. The intention to be open and accepting of resistance towards feelings such as anger, aversion or fear
2. The intention to be aware and resist being pulled by desires including thought, emotions or sensations
3. The intention of kindness, compassion and self-compassion. meaning not to think or act cruelly, violently, or aggressively, and willingness to cultivate kindness for self.

Mindfulness is cultivated effectively within several interrelated and interdependent attitudinal factors, which are non-expectational, patience, non-striving, non-clinging nor aversion to anything that arises in our meditation, remaining impartial, curious, willing to see challenges as opportunities and accept all that arises and learn to let go.

Non-judgmental: When we begin our mindfulness practice, we are likely to discover that we have a constant habit of continuous automatic judgment about our experience. When we experience anything we immediately, and unconsciously, judge and categorize our experience in one of three ways, as, pleasant, unpleasant or neutral. Pleasant events are those which are judged to be good and make us feel good and we want more of them, (attraction or clinging), unpleasant events are judged to be bad and make us feel bad, (aversion or rejection) and neural, of no interest and therefore locked out from our field of awareness.

By adopting an impartial and non-judgmental attitude we create the possibility to see through our own conditioned beliefs, opinions, prejudices and fears and unlock ourselves from our own self-imposed mental and emotional prison.

ਸਭ ਇਕੋ ਹੁਕਮੁ ਵਰਤਦਾ ਮੰਨਿਐ ਸੁਖੁ ਪਾਈ ॥੩॥

Sabh Eiko hukam Varathadhaa Manniai Sukh Paaee ||3||

The hukam is all-pervasive, in acceptance peace is found. ||3||

(Raag Raamkali: Guru Amar Das Ang 948)

Non-expectation and openness: Just as a child is fascinated with a butterfly or a flower when first encountered, approach our meditation session with the same child's-eye. When we sit in meditation we may have conscious or subconscious expectation of relaxing, or having aspecific experience. However, our approach can be one of, no meditation is a bad meditation, and every session of mindfulness is a healing session, irrespective of our experience or expectations.

Curiosity – beginners mind: Have you ever considered what breathing actually is? When we sit there with our focus on the movement of the air into our body and out of our body as the "breath", try to discover what your breath really is.

Non-attachment: In the contextof practising mindfulness, non-attachment can be defined as "Whatever comes, let it come, whatever goes, let it go". Non-attachment consists of becoming aware of the distinction between the object of attachment (pleasures or pains, be it events, sensations, mental impressions, ideas) and the observer. Attachment itself is the root cause of our internal psychological suffering. During our mindfulness practice, emotions, feelings and thoughts will arise with sufficient energetic charge to distract us from our focal point, which is the breath. Neither attached to pleasant events, nor to unpleasant events, simply allowour self to witness "reality" as it arises, rather than howyou wish it to be.

ਮੇਰੇ ਮਨ ਅਹਿਨਿਸਿ ਪੂਰਿ ਰਹੀ ਨਿਤ ਆਸਾ ॥

ਸਤਗੁਰੁ ਸੇਵਿ ਮੋਹੁ ਪਰਜਲੈ ਘਰ ਹੀ ਮਾਹਿ ਉਦਾਸਾ ॥੧॥ਰਹਾਉ॥

Maerae Man Ahinis Poor Rehee Nith Aasaa ||

Sathagur Saev Mohu Parajalai Ghar Hee Maahi
Oudhaasaa ||1|| Rehaao ||

*O my mind, day and night, you are always full of wishful
hopes.*

*Serve the True Guru (Awareness), and your emotional
attachment shall be totally burnt away; remain detached
within the home of your heart. ||1||Pause||*

(Sri Raag Guru Amar Das Ang:29)

Non-aversion and non-clinging: No matter what arises
during our meditation we can adopt an attitude of witnessing
with openness and equality, making our self comfortable with
all that arises.

ਤਿਸਨਾ ਅਗਨਿ ਜਲੈ ਸੰਸਾਰਾ ॥
ਲੋਭੁ ਅਭਿਮਾਨੁ ਬਹੁਤੁ ਅਹੰਕਾਰਾ ॥
ਮਰਿ ਮਰਿ ਜਨਮੈ ਪਤਿ ਗਵਾਏ
ਅਪਣੀ ਬਿਰਥਾ ਜਨਮੁ ਗਵਾਵਣਿਆ ॥੩॥

Thisanaa Agan Jalai Sansaaraa ||

Lobh Abhimaan Bahuth Ahankaaraa ||

Mar Mar Janamai Path Gavaaeae

Apanee Birathhaa Janam Gavaavaniaa ||3||

The world is burning in the fire of desire,
In greed, arrogance and excessive ego.
*People die over and over again; they are re-born, and lose
their dignity wasting their lives in vain. ||3||*

(Raag Maajh Guru Amar Das Ang:120)

Trust: Each one of us is our own authority, yet most
people project their trust upon others, where trusting in the
"authority" of another (be in a doctor, a teacher or politician)
becomes their truth, rather than truth (their own experience,
feelings, intuition) being their authority. Mindfulness helps
cultivate self-trust, trust in oneself, and empowerment. By
practising right-mindfulness you are taking responsibility

for your own wellbeing and health, recognising how the psychological patterns associated with the threat-response can harm our health and how cultivating present moment awareness can undo their harmful impact and restore physiological, psychological and emotional equilibrium. Just as we become aware of one breath at a time, we also begin to recognise the inherent trust in our breath, in the unfolding of our moment by moment, breath by breath experience.

Mindfulness, Naam Symran and transpersonal development

Mindfulness (Symran) is a vital and essential first step towards a safe and methodological process towards inner inquiry, self-realisation and ultimately self-sovereignty. Gurmat provides a highly elegant and refined approach to actualise human potential and then to move beyond the ego.

Naam Symran, the uninterrupted repetition of a specific mantra paced with the breath and accompanied with focusing attention on the sense of self in the chest or Hirdya, provides the systematic self-transformational moving beyond the temporary states of consciousness to permanent stages of consciousness. As one moves through their transpersonal journey and development there are "signposts" or stages and states consciousness identified in the Guru Granth Sahib that provide us with a tantalising invitation to understand this most important of key questions, "what am I?"as part of the process towards self-realisation and ultimately self-sovereignty?

	Awareness	Subjective experience	
Alert	Here and Now	Silence and tranquility	Inner experience of thoughts and emotions
Deep alertness		Acceptance non-judgemental	Non-judgemental openness to experience without control
Deepest	Presence	Aware of current actions, and aware of yourself	Aware of awareness

ਸਤੁ ਸੰਤੋਖੁ ਦਇਆ ਧਰਮੁ ਸਚੁ
ਇਹ ਅਪੁਨੈ ਗ੍ਰਿਹ ਭੀਤਰਿ ਵਾਰੇ ॥੧॥

Sath Santhokh Dhaeiaa Dhharam Sach
Eih Apunai Grih Bheethar Vaarae ||1||

Transparency, contentment, compassion, ethics and
authenticity - I have ushered these into the home of my
self. ||1||

(Raag Asa Guru Arjan Dev Ang:37)

Sach: Gratitude and Humility

Dharm: personal ethics and values

Daya: Compassion and self compassion

Santokh: Contentment – Present moment

Sat: Present Moment, "to be" unchanging, being

The following table outline absorption stages (Gyan) of our meditation practices and describe the experiential qualities present and those absent as we progress in our inner journey:

Gyan stages	Absence	Present	Gurmat Reference
First	Sense desires		
	unwholesome states of mind		
Second		Contentment	Santokh
		unification of mind	Ekagrata
Third	Pleasure	Clearly aware	Sudh man
	suffering	Self-compassion	Dya
		Mindfulness	Ekagrata
Fourth		equanimity	Sahej
		Mindfulness	Ekagrata
Fifth	Bodily sensations	Sphere of Infinite Space	Thhaan Thhananthar
	sense of resistance		Hukam
	perceptions of diversity		Anek
Sixth	Sphere of Infinite Space	Sphere of Infinite Consciousness	Baeant Apaar
Seventh	Sphere of Infinite Consciousness	Sphere of No-thingness	Nirgun
Eight	Sphere of No-thingness	Sphere of Neither Perception nor Non-perception	Akaal

The detailed subject of transpersonal development, its psychology and processes are beyond the scope of this publication and requires a comprehensive and dedicated publication to provide the science behind this most valuable process in the cultivation of human potential.

In summary, Gurmat Psychotherapy is evidence based systematic process of enabling the human being to experience authentic self and can develop and express human potential. This is a serious consciousness based approach to discovering why we are here and what we may become.

Gurmat psychotherapy is a mind-body science which differs from the century old school of Western psychology in several ways: Gurmat Psychotherapy is primarily based on the teachings of the Sikh Gurus, Bhagats and Mystics as contained in Sri Guru Granth Sahib. The Sri Guru Granth Sahib views Existence as sacred non-dual, self-aware Reality (tat). It further provides a deep insight into the highly evolved and sophisticated understanding of the human function, the role of "Haumai", (ego-complex), its cultivation and actualisation to the point of ego-transcendence, Jivan Mukti or self-realisation and self-sovereignty.

Gurmat psychotherapy recognises fundamental distinction between mind and consciousness, as well as distinction between "brain" and "mind". Consciousness as the ground condition of all awareness is a composite of being and knowing.

While Western psychology is primarily focused on "ego-fixing" Gurmat psychotherapy recognises the ego-complex (self-identity system – an active dynamic psychological sense of self), as the source of our suffering as well as its universal projection upon its surroundings, moulding its relationships, destroying its environment and conditioned into a superficial self-gratifying sense of self with a dualistic worldview in which it is easily maintained, manipulated, managed and ultimately controlled.

Gurmat psychotherapy is grounded in both Symran (mindfulness) and its transpersonal dimension Naam Symran, Presence.Gurmat psychotherapy is a safe and practical approach to self-development and ego-transcendence.

Gurmat psychotherapy as a mind-body approach helps cultivate ones identity and intellect (Vivek Buddh) towards a healthy wholesome sense of self and human function in its interaction with the world around one self. Gurmat psychotherapy is a latest offering of the highly evolved human development, evidence rich systems from India and the Far East particularly Buddhism, Aryveda, Yoga, Daoism and Zen.

Gurmat psychotherapy has a clear and concise understanding of the nature of the mind, consciousness, awareness, ego-complex (conditioned sense of self) and the non-dual nature of existence. Gurmat psychotherapypractices that help cultivate an authentic sense of self by recognising and transcending the our identity fused with the content of one's mind, emotions, desires and body (Manmukh) and reveal a self-aware state of consciousness (Gurmukh), our authentic self.

Practices such as Symran (mindfulness) and its transpersonal dimension through Naam Symran are the foundation of Gurmat psychotherapy, which together with additional processes and practices help discover and experience a non-dual, interconnected whole sense of Self, realigning and harmonising the individual dualistic and fragmented self of self towards a unified sacred wholeness.

This publication focuses on providing an outline of the sophisticated psycho-spiritual psychology presented in Sikh thought. This publication has omitted several important elements in Gurmat including Sangat (collective consciousness), congregation of those seeking self-realisation, Nazar, grace, Rehat discipline.

References

1. Misra, Girishwar; Cornelissen, R. M. Matthijs; Verma, Suneet. Foundations of Indian Psychology, Volume 1: Theories and Concepts (Kindle Locations 265-269). Pearson India.

2. Kumar, Manoj, Bhugra, Dinesh, & Singh, Jagmohan (2005) South Asian (Indian) Traditional Healing: Ayurvedic, Shamanic, and Sahaja Therapy in Moodly & West (ed.) Integrating Traditional Healing Practices Into Counselling and Psychotherapy Sage, New Delhi.

3. Encyclopaedia of the History of Psychological Theories Girishwar Misra and Anand C. Paranjpe 2012).

4. Erik Linstrum 2016 Ruling Minds: Psychology in the British Empire . (Cambridge, Mass., Harvard University Press.

5. Laungani, Pittu, D. (2007) A conceptual model of cross-cultural differences in eastern and western cultures in Pittu, D. Laungani (2007) Understanding Cross-Cultural Psychology Sage, New Delhi.

6. Fernando, Suman (2003) Psychiatry and mental health from a Transcultural perspective in Fernando, Suman (2003) Cultural Diversity, Mental Health and Psychiatry: the struggle against racism Brunner- Routeledge, New York.

7. James, W. (1890) The Principles of Psychology, New York: H. Holt.

8. James, W. (1879) "Are We Automata?" Mind, 4: 1–22.

9. Anderson, C.A., Berkowitz, L., Donnerstein, E., Huesmann, L.R., Johnson, J., Linz, D., Malamuth, N., & Wartella, E. (2003). The influence of media violence on youth. Psychological Science in the Public Interest, 4, 81–110. doi: 10.1111/j.1529–1006.2003.pspi_1433.

10. Anderson, C.A., & Bushman, B.J. (2002a). The effects of media violence on society. Science, 295, 2377–2378. doi: 10.1126/science.1070765 prosocial behavior in Eastern and Western countries. Psychological Bulletin, 136, 151–173.

11. Anderson, C.A., & Bushman, B.J. (2002b). Human aggression. Annual Review of Psychology,53, 27–51. doi: 10.1146/annurev.psych.53.100901.135231.

13. Lene Arnett Jensen, Bridging Cultural and Developmental Approaches to Psychology, New Syntheses in Theory, Research, and Policy, 2010, Oxford University Press.

12. Anderson, C.A., Shibuya, A., Ihori, N., Swing, E.L., Bushman, B.J., Sakamoto, A., Rothstein, H.R., & Saleem, M. (2010). Violent video game effects on aggression, empathy, and

14. David J. Chalmers, 1997 Facing Up to the Problem of Consciousness, in Explaining Consciousness, The hard problem, Jonathan Shear.

15. Curley, E. M., 1978. Descartes Against the Sceptics, Cambridge, MA: Harvard University Press.
1986. "Analysis in the Meditations: The Quest for Clear and Distinct Ideas," in Essays on Descartes' Meditations, ed. Amélie Oksenberg Rorty, Berkeley: University of California Press.

16. Curley, E. M., 1993. "Certainty: Psychological, Moral, and Metaphysical," in Essays on the Philosophy and Science of René Descartes, ed. Stephen Voss, Oxford: Oxford University Pres.

17. JA Gray. The Neuropsychohgy of Anxiety: An Enquiry into the Functions of the Septo-Hippocampal System. 2nd ed. New York, NY: Oxford University Press; 2003.

18. Christina D Steel, Mayumi Machida, Patric S Lundberg, Laurie Wellman, Larry D Sanford and Richard P Ciavarra J Immunol Stress perception differentially regulates the inflammatory response in the CNS to a neurotropic viral pathogen May 1, 2016, 196 (1 Supplement) 217.2;

19. Jerath, R., Edry J.W, Barnes, V.A., and Jerath, V. (2006). Physiology of long pranayamic breathing: Neural respiratory

elements may provide a mechanism that explains how slow deep breathing shifts the autonomic nervous system. Medical Hypothesis, 67, 566-571.

20. Wakefield, Jerome CDisorder as harmful dysfunction: A conceptual critique of DSM-III-R's definition of mental disorder.. Psychological Review, Vol 99(2), Apr 1992, 232-247.

21. Robert B. Cialdini, Influence: The Psychology of Persuasion, Revised Edition Revised Edition 1984.

22. Muller, Charles (2004). The Yogâcâra Two Hindrances and Their Reinterpretations in East Asia. Toyo Gakuen University. Source: http://www.acmuller.net/articles/reinterpretations_of_ the_hindrances.html(accessed: January 5, 2008).

23. Lisa Dale Miller, Effortless Mindfulness: Genuine Mental Health Through Awakened Presence, Routledge, 2014.

24. Padgett, David A. et al. How stress influences the immune response,Trends in Immunology , Volume 24 , Issue 8 , 444-448.

25. Khovidhunkit, W, et al. Effects of infection and inflammation on lipid and lipoprotein metabolism: mechanisms and consequences to the host [review]. J. Lipid Res. 2004. 45:1169-1196.

26. Kathryn E. Wellen and Gökhan S. Hotamisligil, Inflammation, stress, and diabetes American Society for Clinical Investigation, First published May 2, 2005.

27. Astin JA, Shapiro SL, Eisenberg DM, Forys KL (2003) Mind–body medicine: state of the science, implications for practice. J Am Board Fam Pract 16: 131–147 [PubMed].

28. Padgett DA, Glaser R (2003) How stress influences the immune response. Trends Immunol 24: 444–448.

29. Vicki Brower, Mind–body research moves towards the mainstream, European Molecular Biology Organization, 2006.

30. Shirley Telles, Patricia Gerbarg, and Elisa H. Kozasa, Physiological Effects of Mind and Body Practices, Hindawi Publishing Corporation BioMed Research International Volume 2015.

31. Christopher J. Patrick, Greg Hajcak, Reshaping clinical science: Introduction to the Special Issue on *Psychophysiology and the NIMH Research Domain Criteria (RDoC) initiative* Authors.

32. Bryant, Richard A.; Harvey, Allison G.; Guthrie, Rachel M.; Moulds, Michelle L.,,A prospective study of psychophysiological arousal, acute stress disorder, and posttraumatic stress disorder Journal of Abnormal Psychology, Vol 109(2), May 2000, 341-344.

33. Rosen, Raymond C.; Beck, J. Gayle, Patterns of sexual arousal: Psychophysiological processes and clinical applications.
New York, NY, US: Guilford Press Patterns of sexual arousal: Psychophysiological processes and clinical applications. (1988)

34. GJ Norman, E Necka, GG Berntson - The Psychophysiology of Emotions, Emotion Measurement, 2016.

35. Ruud Hortensius, Beatrice de Gelder, Dennis J. L. G. Schutter, When anger dominates the mind: Increased motor corticospinal excitability in the face of threat John Wiley & Sons, Ltd 2016.

36. Wolkow, A., Aisbett, B., Reynolds, J. et al. Acute Psychophysiological Relationships Between Mood, Inflammatory and Cortisol Changes in Response to Simulated Physical Firefighting Work and Sleep Restriction, Appl Psychophysiology Biofeedback, 2016, Volume 41, Issue 2, pp 165–180.

37. Kirschner, Hans, Compassion for the Self and Well-Being: Psychological and Biological Correlates of a New Concept, University of Exeter 2016.

38. Richardson, M., McEwan, K., Maratos, F. et al. ,Joy and Calm: How an Evolutionary Functional Model of Affect Regulation Informs Positive Emotions in Nature, Evolutionary Psychological Science (2016).

39. Firdaus Dhabhar, Stress, anxiety, and susceptibility to squamous cell carcinoma: Role of immune mediators, Psychoneuroendocrinology, Volume 71, 1 - 2.

40. Compton, William C,Introduction to Positive Psychology. Belmont, CA, US: Thomson Wadsworth Introduction to Positive Psychology.(2005).

41. Gholam Reza Nikrahan, Ph.D., Johannes A.C. Laferton, Ph.D., Karim Asgari, Ph.D., Mehrdad Kalantari, Ph.D., Mohammad Reza Abedi, Ph.D., Ali Etesampour, M.D., Abbas Rezaei, Ph.D., Laura Suarez, M.D., Jeff C. Huffman, M.D. Effects of Positive Psychology Interventions on Risk Biomarkers in Coronary Patients, The Academy of Psychosomatic Medicine. Published by Elsevier Inc. 2016.

42. Ojanperä, I., Kriikku, P. & Vuori, E. Int J, Fatal toxicity index of medicinal drugs based on a comprehensive toxicology database, Legal Med (2016) 130: 1209.

43. Donald, James N., et al. "Daily stress and the benefits of mindfulness: Examining the daily and longitudinal relations between present-moment awareness and stress responses." *Journal of Research in Personality* 65 (2016): 30-37.

44. Van Cappellen, Patty, et al. "Religion and well-being: The mediating role of positive emotions." *Journal of Happiness studies* 17.2 (2016): 485-505.

45. Vanlessen, Naomi, et al. "Happy heart, smiling eyes: a systematic review of positive mood effects on broadening of visuospatial attention." *Neuroscience & Biobehavioral Reviews* 68 (2016): 816-837.

46. Reed, Rebecca G., et al. "Emotional acceptance, inflammation, and sickness symptoms across the first two years following breast cancer diagnosis." *Brain, behavior, and immunity* 56 (2016): 165-174.

47. Amaranath, B., Hongasandra R. Nagendra, and Sudheer Deshpande. "Effect of integrated Yoga module on positive and negative emotions in Home Guards in Bengaluru: A wait list randomized control trial." *International journal of yoga* 9.1 (2016): 35.

48. Sinclair, Shane, et al. "Compassion in health care: An empirical model." *Journal of pain and symptom management* 51.2 (2016): 193-203.

49. Gautam, S., et al. "Impact of Meditation and Yoga on Oxidative DNA Damage in Sperm: Clinical Implications." *J Yoga Phys Ther* 6.250 (2016): 2.

50. Yoo, Yang-Gyeong, et al. "The effects of mind subtraction meditation on depression, social anxiety, aggression, and salivary cortisol levels of elementary school children in South Korea." *Journal of pediatric nursing* 31.3 (2016): e185-e197.

51. Choi, Kyung Mook. "The impact of organokines on insulin resistance, inflammation, and atherosclerosis." *Endocrinology and Metabolism* 31.1 (2016): 1-6.

52. Millstein, Rachel A., et al. "The effects of optimism and gratitude on adherence, functioning and mental health following an acute coronary syndrome." *General Hospital Psychiatry* 43 (2016): 17-22.

53. Shao, Di, Wen Gao, and Feng-Lin Cao. "Brief psychological intervention in patients with cervical cancer: A randomized controlled trial." *Health Psychology* 35.12 (2016): 1383.

54. Garland, Eric L., et al. "Linking dispositional mindfulness and positive psychological processes in cancer survivorship: a multivariate path analytic test of the mindfulness to meaning theory." *Psycho Oncology* (2016).

55. Moreno, Patricia I., et al. "Positive affect and inflammatory activity in breast cancer survivors: examining the role of affective arousal." *Psychosomatic medicine* 78.5 (2016): 532-541.

56. Laster Pirtle, Whitney N., and Tony N. Brown. "Inconsistency within Expressed and Observed Racial Identifications: Implications for Mental Health Status." *Sociological Perspectives* 59.3 (2016): 582-603.

57. Soller, Brian, Dana L. Haynie, and Alena Kuhlemeier. "Sexual intercourse, romantic relationship inauthenticity, and adolescent mental health." *Social Science Research* (2016).

58. Millstein, Rachel A., et al. "The effects of optimism and gratitude on adherence, functioning and mental health following an acute coronary syndrome." *General Hospital Psychiatry* 43 (2016): 17-22.

59. Jiang, Feng, et al. "How belief in a just world benefits mental health: The effects of optimism and gratitude." *Social Indicators Research* 126.1 (2016): 411-423.

60. Kok, B. E., et al. "Corrigendum: How Positive Emotions Build Physical Health: Perceived Positive Social Connections Account for the Upward Spiral Between Positive Emotions and Vagal Tone." *Psychological Science* 27.6 (2016): 931.

61. Fredrickson, Barbara L. *Handbook of positive emotions*. Eds. Michele M. Tugade, Michelle N. Shiota, and Leslie D. Kirby. Guilford Publications, 2016.

62. Richmond, Kacy, Erin Zerbo, and Petros Levounis. "What Is Mindfulness?." *Becoming Mindful: Integrating Mindfulness Into Your Psychiatric Practice* (2016): 1.

63. Young, Shinzen. "What Is Mindfulness? A Contemplative Perspective." *Handbook of Mindfulness in Education*. Springer New York, 2016. 29-45.

64. Eaton, Marie. "NAVIGATING ANGER, FEAR, GRIEF, AND DESPAIR." *Contemplative Approaches to Sustainability in Higher Education: Theory and Practice* (2016).

65. Harpin, Scott B., et al. "Behavioral Impacts of A Mindfulness Pilot Intervention For Elementary School Students." *Oldest Journal in the United States* 137.2 (2016): 149.

66. Carter, Kirtigandha Salwe, and Robert Carter III. "Breath-based meditation: A mechanism to restore the physiological and cognitive reserves for optimal human performance." *World journal of clinical cases* 4.4 (2016): 99.

67. Shackle, Christopher, and Arvind Mandair, eds. *Teachings of the Sikh Gurus: Selections from the Sikh Scriptures*. Routledge, 2013

68. Singh, Pashaura, and Louis E. Fenech. *The Oxford handbook of Sikh studies*. Oxford University Press, 2014.

69. Mandair, Arvind-Pal S., Christopher Shackle, and Gurharpal Singh. *Sikh religion, culture and ethnicity*. Routledge, 2013.
70. Mandair, Arvind-pal. "Thinking differently about religion and history: Issues for Sikh studies." *Sikh religion, culture and ethnicity* (2001).
71. Mandair, Arvind-pal Singh. *Religion and the specter of the West: Sikhism, India, postcoloniality, and the politics of translation*. Columbia University Press, 2013.
72. Singh, Kala. "The Sikh spiritual model of counseling." *Spirituality and Health International* 9.1 (2008): 32-43.
73. Stoeber, Michael. "3HO Kundalini Yoga and Sikh Dharma." *Sikh Formations* 8.3 (2012): 351-368.
74. Chilana, Rajwant Singh. "Sikh Code of Conduct, Institutions & Ceremonies." (2005): 295-310.
75. Macauliffe, Max Arthur. *The Sikh Religion: Its Gurus, Sacred Writings and Authors*. Vol. 6. Cambridge University Press, 2013.
76. Kala Singh,The Sikh spiritual model of counselling,Spirituality and Health International 9:32–43 (2008) Published online 12 December 2007 in Wiley InterScience.
77. Nabha, Kahan Singh Ji, *Gurushabad Ratanakar Mahan Kosh* [Reprint]. Patiala, 1981.

Glossary

Abhimani: Egotistic sense of self

Acheta: Unintelligent.

Achetana: Unconscious.

Achintya: Unthinkable.

Adharma: All that is contrary to the right and the law; demerit.

Adhi: Disease of the mind.

Advaita: Non-duality; Brahman is the only existence.

Advitiya: Without a second.

Agni: Fire.

Aham: I; the ego.

Aham Atma: I am the Atman.

Aham Brahmasmi: I am Brahman.

Aham karta: I am the doer.

Ahamkara: Egoism or self-conceit; the self-arrogating principle 'I', 'I am'-ness; self-consciousness. *Rajasika ahamkara:* Dynamic egoism with passion and pride. *Sattvika ahamkara:* Egoism composed in the sense of goodness and virtue. *Tamasika ahamkara:* Egoism as expressed in ignorance and inertia.

Ajapa: The Mantra "Soham" (I am He) which is produced by the breath itself, without any conscious effort at repeating it: the inhalation sounding 'So' and the exhalation 'ham'.

Ajapa-gayatri: Hamsah-soham Mantra.

Ajapa-japa: Japa of "Soham" Mantra.

Ajayan: Ignorance.

Akhar: The first letter or the most fundamental sound which is represented by the first letter of the alphabet.

Amrit: Nectar.

Amritam: Immortality.

Amrita-nadi: A special psychic nerve branching from the heart.

Amritattva: Deathlessness; immortality.

Anaham: 'Not-I'; non-ego.

Anahata: The fourth lotus of the Yogis, opposite the heart; mystic sounds heard by the Yogis.

Ananda: Non-dual sense experienced as bliss, happiness; joy.

Anandamaya Kosa: Blissful sheath or Karana Sarira, the seed body which contains Mula Ajnana or the potentialities.

Anandamaya: Full of bliss.

Ananyata: Single-mindedness.

Aneka: Not one but multiplicity.

Annamaya kosa: Food-sheath; gross physical body.

Antahkarana: Internal instrument; fourfold mind; mind (thought), intellect (discrimination), I- am-ness and memory.

Antahkarana-chatushtaya: The mind in its four aspects, viz., Manas, Buddhi, Chitta and Ahamkara; fourfold internal organ.

Antahkarana-sastra: Psychology; science of the internal organ, viz., mind, intelligence and ego.

Antar: Internal; middle; interspace.

Antaranga: Internal organ; mind.

Antar-drishti: Inner vision.

Apana: The nerve-current which governs the abdominal region, which has its centre in the anus; it does excretory function of the faecal matter; it works for ejection; the down-going breath.

Artha: Meaning; sense; purpose; object; object of perception; an object of desire; wealth.

Arupa: Formless.

Asanga: Non-attachment.

Asat: That which is not; non-existent; non-being as opposed to Sat or Being or existence or Reality; unreal.

Asmita: Egoism; I-ness; "am"-ness.

Asthula: Without grossness; subtle; Brahman.

Asti: Exists; is; Brahman.

Atma (also, Atman): The Self.

Atma-Gyan: Knowledge of the Self

Atma-chintana: Reflection on the Self or the A tman.

Atma-drishti: The vision of seeing everything as the Self.

Atma-jnana: Direct knowledge of the Self; Brahma-jnana.

Avidya: Ignorance; nescience; an elusive power within Existence (Brahman) which is sometimes regarded as one with Maya and sometimes as different from it. It forms the condition of the individual consciousness.

Baddha: Bound; one who is in a state of bondage.

Bandha: Bondage; tie or knot;

Bandha-moksha: Bondage and liberation.

Bhakti: Devotion; love (of God).

Bhakti-marga: The path of devotion to attain divinity.

Bhandara: Storehouse.

Bhava: mental attitude, feeling; subjective state of being; attitude of mind; state of realisation in the heart or mind; right feeling and frame of mind; right intention; right imagination; right mental disposition; purity of thought. Any of the five such attitudes as

Santa, Dasya, Sakhya, Vatsalya and Madhurya (of peace, of servant, of friend, of maternal, and of a lover, respectively.

Bhavana: Feeling; mental attitude.

Bhay: Fear.

Bheda-ahamkara: The differentiating ego; sense of separateness.

Bheda-buddhi: The intellect that creates differences, the Vyavaharika Buddhi that diversifies everything as opposed to Paramarthika Buddhi that unifies everything..

Bheda-jnana: Consciousness of difference; worldly consciousness.

Bhoga: Experience; perception; enjoyment.

Bhram: Illusion; delusion; rotation; wandering.

Bija: Seed; source.

Bijakshara: The root-letter or the seed-letter in which there is the latent power of a Mantra.

Bijatma: The subtle inner Self-, also called Sukshmatma, Sutratma or Antaryamin.

Bodha: Spiritual wisdom; knowledge; intelligence.

Brahma: God as creator; the first of the created beings. Hiranyagarbha or cosmic intelligence.

Brahma-bhava(na): Feeling of identity with Brahman, as well as of everything as Brahman.

Brahman: Satchitananda, the Absolute Reality; the Supreme Reality that is one and indivisible, infinite, and eternal; all-pervading, changeless Existence; Existence-knowledge-bliss Absolute; the substratum of Jiva, Isvara and Maya; Absolute Consciousness; it is not only all-powerful but all-power itself; not only all-knowing and blissful, but all-knowledge and bliss itself.

Buddha: The enlightened one; full of knowledge.

Buddhi: Intellect, discrimination; understanding; reason.

Buddhi-sakti: Intellectual power.

Chaitanya: The consciousness that knows itself an knows others; absolute consciousness.

Chaitanya-samadhi: The state of superconsciousness which is marked by absolute self-awareness and illumination

Chakra: Plexus; centre of psychic energy in the human system.

Chetas: Subconscious mind.

Chidabhasa: Reflected consciousness; the reflection of intelligence (Jiva).

Chit-ananda: Consciousness-Bliss.

Chinta: Anxiety, suffering; worry.

Chintana: Thinking; reflecting.

Chit: The principle of universal intelligence or consciousness.

Chitta: Mind-stuff; subconscious mind.

Daan: Charity; giving.

Darna: Control of the outer senses; one of the sixfold virtues of the Niyama of Raja Yoga..

Darsan: Insight; way of seeing; vision; system of philosophy; making visible.

Daya: Mercy; compassion.

Dehi: Physical body.

Dehabhimana: Egoistic attachment to the body.

Dehadhyasa: False identification with the body.

Dehi: One who has a body; the conscious embodied self; Jiva

Dhara: Stream; continuous repetition.

Dharana: Concentration of mind.

Dharma: Ethical way of living, as enjoined by the sacred scriptures; characteristics; virtue.

Dhyana: Mindfulness Meditation; contemplation.

Diksha: Initiation; consecration.

Duhkh: Suffering, Pain; misery; sorrow; grief.

Dvaita-bhava: Feeling of duality.

Dvesha: Repulsion; hatred; dislike.

Eka: One.

Ekabhavika: Unigenital; uninatal; of the same source or nature.

Ekagrata: One-pointedness of the mind; concentration,

Ekata: Oneness; homogeneity; absoluteness.

Gambhir: Deep; magnanimous; dignified; grand; imperious; grave.

Gati: State; movement; going.

Granthi: Tie or knot, one who is enlightened

Grihastha: Householder.

Gufa: Cave.

Guna: Quality born of nature.

Gunamaya: Full of qualities or attributes.

Gunasamya: A state where the three Gunas are found in equilibrium; the Supreme Absolute.

Guru: Teacher; preceptor.

Gurukripa: Preceptor's grace or blessings.

Gurumantra: Mantra in which one has been initiated by the Guru, the third form of God, Nirgun or unmanifest, Sargun or Manifest and Gurmantra.

Hari: A being who destroys the evil deeds of those who take refuge in Him. A name of God Existence.

Hridaya: Heart; essential centre on the right hand side, spiritual heart.

Hridayagufa: The cave or chamber of the heart.

Hridayakamala: Lotus of the heart.

Iccha: Desire.

Ida: The psychic nerve-current flowing through the left nostril; it is the cooling lunar Nadi as distinguished from Pingala, the heating solar Nadi.

Indriya: The sense of perception; sense-organ; this either the physical external Karma-Indriya (organ of action) or the internal Jnana-Indriya (organ of knowledge, cognition or perception).

Indriyajnana: Sense-knowledge or perception.

Isht: Object of desire; the chosen ideal; the particular form of God that one is devoted to; a sacrificial rite.

Isht-mantra: The Mantra of the chosen or tutelary deity.

Jagadguru: World preceptor.

Jagat: Space and Time containing Universe, continiously changing.

Jagrat: Waking condition.

Japa: Repetition of God's Name again and again; repetition of a Mantra.

Japamaala: Rosary (to count the number of repetitio done).

Jiva: Individual Embodied consciousness with ego.

Jivachaitanya: Individual consciousness.

Jivanmukta: One who is liberated in this life.

Jivanmukti: Liberated in this life, while yet living.

Jivatma: Individual embodied consciousness.

Jnana: Knowledge; wisdom of the Reality or Brahman, Absolute.

Kaal: Time; death or yesterday, tomorrow.

Kaalachakra: Wheel of time.

Kaliyuga: Age of Kali, age of ignorance, dominated by self of "I"-am ness and ignorant of sacredness of self and Existence ; iron age; the last of the four Yugas; the present age; the dark, evil age.

Kalpana: Imagination of the mind; mental creation.

Kalpanamatra: Mere imagination; resting only in imagination.

Kalpanika: That which is imagined; falsely created.

Kama: Desire; passion; lust.

Kanda: The root; the source of all Nadis; the egg-shaped centre of nerves located below the region of the navel.

Kanth: Throat; neck.

Karan: Cause; reason; the unmanifested potential cause that, in due time, takes shape as the visible effect; the material cause of the universe in such a state during the period of dissolution, i.e., cosmic energy in a potential condition.

Karana-jagat: Causal world.

Karana-sarira: The causal body (where the individual rests during sound, deep, dreamless sleep, the intellect, mind and senses being reduced to an unmanifested potential condition); this is the proximate cover of "essence", known as the sheath of bliss.

Karma: Action. It is of three kinds: *Sanchita* (all the accumulated actions of all previous births), *Prarabdha* (the particular portion of such Karma allotted for being worked out in this present life), and *Agami* (current Karma being freshly performed by the individual). It is the Karma operating through the law of cause and effect binding the Jiva or the individual consciousness to the wheel of birth and death fused with imprints created through a sense of "I" amness.

Karmabandha: Bondage caused by Karma.

Karmendriya: Organ of action: tongue (speech), hands, feet, eyes (sight), ears (sound) genital and anus are the organs of action.

Karta: Doer; the subject of action.

Karuna: Mercy; compassion; kindness.

Karya: Effect (correlative of Karana); the physical body described as the Karya, in contrast to the causal body, the Karana; the world; Hiranyagarbha.

Katha: Tale or story; history or narrative.

Kaya: Physical body.

Khalsa: Pure, egoless, self-actualised, self-realised and self-sovereign human being, Sky; ether.

Klesa: Affliction; pain.

Kosa: Sheath; bag; scabbard; a sheath enclosing the soul; there are five such concentric sheaths or the chambers one above the other, namely, the sheaths of bliss, intellect, mind, life-force and the gross body.

Kripa: Mercy; grace; blessing.

Kriya: Physical action; particular exercises in Hath Yoga, such as Basti, Neti, Nauli, etc.

Kriyadvaita: Oneness in action or practical living of Oneness.

Krodha: Anger; wrath.

Krurata: Cruelty; pitilessness.

Khama: Forgiveness.

Kundalini: The primordial cosmic energy located in the individual; it lies coiled up like a serpent with three and a half coils, with head downwards at the basal Muladharachakra.

Laya: Dissolution; merging.

Lila: Play; sport; the cosmos looked upon as a divine play.

Lingasarira: The subtle or psychic body that become particularly active during the dream state by creating a world of its own; the three sheaths of intelligence, mind and vital energy constitute this body.

Lobha: Covetousness; greed.

Loka: World of names and forms

Maala: Rosary; beads used for counting the number of Japa done.

Madhyama: A slightly gross form of sound.

Mahan: The Great

Mahatma: Great consciousness; saint; sage.

Mahavakya: (lit.) Great sentence. Upanishadic declarations, four in number, expressing the highest Vedantic truths or the identity between the individual soul and the Supreme Soul. They are:
1. *Prajnanam Brahma* (Consciousness is Brahman) in Aitareya Upanishad of the Rig Veda.
2. *Aham Brahmasmi* (I am Brahman) in Brihadaranyaka Upanishad of Yajur Veda.
3. *Tat Tvam Asi* (That thou art) in Chhandogya Upanishad of Sama Veda.
4. *Ayam Atma Brahma* (This Self is Brahman) in Mandukya Upanishad of Atharva Veda.

Maitri: Friendliness.

Maal:conditioned mind Impurity of the mind; one of the three defects of the mind.

Mamakara: Mineness; the thought "this is mine" in relation to the body and the things connected with it, such as wife, children, relations, friends, home, wealth and the like.

Mamata: Mineness.

Mana: Respect; sense of self-respect.

Manas: Mind; the thinking faculty, thought.

Manasika: Mental; pertaining to the mind.

Manasikajapa: Mental repetition of a Mantra.

Manasikakriya: Mental action.

Manasisakti: Power of mind; intelligence; understanding.

Mandala: Region; sphere or plane, e.g., Suryaman or the solar region.

Mantra: Sacred syllable or word or set of words through the repetition and reflection of which one attains perfection or realisation of the Self.

Mantra-chaitanya: The dormant potency of Mantra.

Mantra-sakti: Power and potency of any Mantra.

Mantra-siddhi: Perfection in the practice of Mantrajapa; mastery over the Devata of a Mantra so that the Devata graces the votary whenever invoked.

Marga: Path; road.

Maya: The illusive power of Brahman; the veiling and the projecting power of the universe.

Mithya: False; unreal; illusory.

Moha: Infatuation; delusion caused by wrong thinking; false identification and deluded attachment.

Moksha: Release; liberation; the term is particularly applied to the liberation from the bondage of Karma and the wheel of birth and death; Absolute Experience.

Mudra: A certain class of exercises in Hatha Yoga; symbols shown in hands during worship.

Mukta: The liberated one.

Mul or Mool: Origin; root; base.

Mulmantra: Root Mantra, contained in the first verse of Sri Guru Granth Sahib. (ikk ōankār sat(i)-nām(u) karatā purakh(u) nirabha'u niravair(u) akāl(a) mūrat(i) ajūnī saibhan gur(a) prasād(i).
"One creator, sustainer, destroyer, unchanging in nature, creative consciouness, Beyond Fear, Beyond Hatred, Beyond Death, Beyond Birth, Self-Existent, by the Guru's Grace";); the powerful and the most important of the Mantras of any deity.

Murkh: Fool.

Nabhi: Navel.

Nada: Mystic sound (of the Eternal); the primal sound or First vibration from which all creation has emanated; the first manifestation of the unmanifested Absolute; Omkara or Sabda Brahman; also the mystic inner sound or Anahata on which the Yogi concentrates.

Nadi: Nerve; channel; psychic current.

Naam: Name, Presence, Unfolding nature of Nowness.

Namarupa: Name and form; the nature of the world.

Namarupajagat: The world of names and forms.

Nimrata: Humility.

Neti-neti: "Not this, not this"; the analytical process of progressively negating all names and forms in order to arrive at the eternal underlying Truth.

Nidra: Sleep; either dreaming or deep sleep state; also a name of Yogamaya..

Nirankar: Formless.

Niralamba: Supportless.

Niramaya: Without disease.

Niranjana: Spotless.

Niravarana: Without veil, unconditioned.

Nirbhay: Fearless.

Nirguna: Without attribute.

Nirlipta: Unattached.

Nirmala: Without impurity; pure.

Nirmama: Without mine-ness.

Nirmanachitta: Manufactured mind; manufacturing mind.

Nirvana: conditioned mind, Liberation; final emancipation.

Nirvicharasamadhi: Superconscious state where there is no intellectual enquiry.

Nirvikalpa: Without the modifications of the mind.

Nirvikalpasamadhi: The superconscious state where there is no mind or the triad, viz., knower, known and knowledge, or any idea whatsoever.

Nirvikara: Unchanging; without modifications.

Nischay-avritti: The Vritti or state of mind where there is determination.

Nishkama: Without desire.

Nishkama: Action without expectation of fruits.

Nitya-buddhi: Idea of stability; the intellect that considers the world as real.

Om: The Pranava or the sacred syllable symbolising Creation, growth, dissolution infinitum.

Ongkar: Same as Om.

Pada: Foot; one-fourth portion.

Padartha: Substance; material.

Pancha: Five.

Panchakosa: Five sheaths of ignorance enveloping the Self.

Panchakshara: Mantra of Lord Siva, consisting of five letters, viz., (Om) Na-mah-si-va-ya.

Papa: Sin; a wicked action; evil; demerit.

Para: Supreme; other; enemy.

Param-brahma: The Supreme Absolute; the transendental Reality.

Parama: Highest; Supreme.

Paramadhama: Supreme Abode; Brahman, Moksha

Paramananda: Supreme Bliss.

Paramapada: Supreme state; Moksha.

Paramarthadrishti: Right vision; intuition.

Paramatma: The Supreme Self.

Paramesvara: The Supreme Godliness.

Paramjyotih: Supreme Light; Brahman.

Para sabda: Supreme sound which is in an undifferentiated state; the first Avyakta state of sound.

Parayana: The ultimate ground; the sole refuge.

Parispanda: Vibration.

Pavan: Breath, wind .

Pingala: A Nadi or psychic nerve current which terminates in the right nostril; it is the solar Nadi; it is heating in its effect.

Prabuddha: Awakened; conscious of the Ultimate Reality.

Prahar: A period of roughly three hours' duration.

Prajna: Consciousness; awareness.

Prajnanaghana: Mass of consciousness; Brahman.

Prajnatma: The intelligent self; the conscious internal self.

Prakas: Luminosity; light; brightness.

Prakata: Manifest; revealed.

Prana: Vital energy; life-breath; life-force.

Pranamaya: One of the sheaths of the Self, consisting of the Pranas and the Karmendriyas.

Pranasakti: Subtle vital power.

Prasvasa: Expiratory breath.

Prema: Divine love (for God).

Premabhava: Feeling of love.

Punya: Merit; virtue.

Puraka: Inspiration; inhalation of breath.

Purusha: The Supreme Being Consciouness; a Being that lies in the city (of the heart of all beings). The term is applied to God. The description applies to the Self which abides in the heart of all things. To distinguish Bhagavan or the Lord from the Jivatma, He is known as Parama (Highest) Akal Purekh or the Paratama.

Rachana: Creation; construction.

Raga: Blind love; attraction; attachment that binds the soul to the universe.

Raga-dvesha: Attraction and repulsion; like and dislike; love and hatred.

Rajas: One of the three aspects or component traits of cosmic energy; the principle of dynamism in nature bringing about all changes; through this is protected the relative appearance of the Absolute as the universe; this quality generates passion and restlessness.

Rajayoga: A system of Yoga; the royal Yoga of meditation; the system of Yoga generally taken to be the one propounded by Patanjali Maharshi, i.e., the Ashtanga Yoga.

Rasa: Essence (of enjoyment); water; mercury; taste; sweet feeling; food-chyle; Brahman.

Rasana: Tongue; the organ of taste.

Rupa: Appearance; form; sight; vision.

Sabda: Sound; word; Ongkar/Omkar.

Sabdabrahma: Word-Absolute; Ongkar/Omkar.

Sabdatanmatra: Subtle principle of sound.

Sabha: Assembly.

Satchidananda: Existence-knowledge-bliss Absolute. (Also, Sat-chit-ananda.)

Sadajagrat: Ever wakeful.

Sadbhashana: Right speech.

Sadhu: Pious or righteous man; a Sannyasin.

Sahaj: Natural, harmonious; true; native.

Sahaja-kumbhaka: Natural retention of breath.

Sahajananda: State of bliss that has become natural.

Sahaja-nirvikalpa-samadhi: Natural non-dual state of Brahmic Consciousness.

Sahajanishtha: Natural and normal establishment; establishment in one's own essential nature of Satchidananda.

Sakti: Power; energy; force; the Divine Power of becoming; the apparent dynamic aspect of Eternal Being; the Absolute Power or cosmic energy.

Samadhi: The state of superconsciousness where Absoluteness is experienced attended with all-knowledge and joy; Oneness; here the mind becomes identified with the object of meditation; the meditator and the meditated, thinker and thought become one in perfect absorption of the mind.

Samata: Balanced state of mind.

Samjnana: To know intellectually.

Sampradaya: Sect; custom; conventional procedure or course of action.

Samsara: Life through repeated births and deaths; the process of worldly life.

Samsari: The transmigrating soul.

Sanatana-dharma: Eternal Religion.

Sanga: Attachment; company.

Sankalpa: Thought, desire; imagination.

Sankalpamatra: Mere thought; existing in thought only.

Sankocha: Contraction; involution; hesitation.

Santosh: Contentment; joy; happiness.

Sannyasi (or Sannyasin): A monk; one who has embraced the life of complete renunciation; one belonging to the fourth or the highest stage of life, viz., Sannyasa.

Sarira: Body.

Sattva: Light; purity; reality.

Sattvaguna: Quality of light, purity and goodness.

Satya: Truth; Brahman or the Absolute.

Satyatva: State of Truth.

Seva: Service.

Shad-urmi: Six waves, viz., grief, delusion, hunger, thirst, decay and death.

Shad-vikara: Six modifications of the body, viz., existence, birth, growth, change, decay and death.

Siddha: Realised; perfected; a perfected Yogi.

Sikh: Student, state of not knowing wanting to learn, follower of the teachings o Sikh Gurus .

Smarana: Remembrance, Mindfulness, Nowness, here.

Smarta: Pertaining to or enjoined by the Smriti.

Smriti: Memory; code of law.

Sparsa: Touch; feeling with skin.

Sparsatanmatra: The essence of the sense of touch..

Sraddha: trust.

Sri: Supreme.

Srishti: Creation.

Sukha: Pleasure; happiness; joy.

Sukhachintana: Thought of happiness; happy thinking.

Sukh: Happiness

Sunya: Void; nothingness; zeroness; vacuity; nullity.

Sushupti: Deep sleep without dreams.

Sutra: Thread; string; an aphorism with minimum words and maximum sense; a terse sentence.

Svara: Sound; accent; tone.

Svasa: Breath.

Teen taap: Sufferings or afflictions of three kinds, to which mortals are subject, viz., (1) those caused by one's own body (Adhyatmika), (2) those caused by beings around him (Adhibhautika), and (3) those caused by Devas (Adhidaivika).

Tamas: Ignorance; inertia; darkness; perishability.

Tandra: Drowsiness; half-sleepy state; an obstacle in meditation.

Tantra: A manual of or a particular path of Sadhana laying great stress upon Japa of a Mantra and other esoteric Upasanas.

Tapas: Purificatory action; ascetic self-denial; austerity; penance; mortification.

Taranga: Wave.

Tattva: Reality; element; truth; essence; principle.

Tripti: Satisfaction

Trishna: Thirsting (for objects); internal craving (for sense-objects).

Tyaga: Renunciation (of egoism and Vasanas, and the world).

Udasina: Indifferent.

Udasinata: Indifference (to objects and sense-attractions); state of being indifferent.

Unmanibhava: Mindlessness.

Upadhi: A superimposed thing or attribute that veils and gives a coloured view of the substance beneath it; limiting adjunct;

instrument; vehicle; body; a technical term used in Vedanta philosophy for any superimposition that gives a limited view of the Absolute and makes It appear as the relative. Jiva's Upadhi is Avidya; Isvara's Upadhi is Maya.

Vach: Speech.

Vachya: That which is denoted by speech.

Vaikhari japa: Articulate or loud repetition of a Mantra.

Vasana: Subtle desire; a tendency created in a person by the doing of an action or by enjoyment; it induces the person to repeat the action or to seek a repetition of the enjoyment; the subtle impression in the mind capable of developing itself into action; it is the cause of birth and experience in general; the impression of actions that remains unconsciously in the mind.

Vastu: Object; substance; Brahman.

Vata: Wind; one of the three humours of the body; rheumatism.

Vedanasakti: Power of cognition or sensation.

Vega: Momentum; force.

Vichara: Enquiry into the nature of the Self, Brahman or Truth; ever-present reflection on the why and wherefore of things; enquiry into the real meaning of the Gurbani; discrimination between the Real and the unreal; enquiry of Self.

Vidya: Knowledge (of Brahman); there are two kinds of knowledge, Paravidya and Aparavidya; a process of meditation or worship.

Vikalpa: Imagination; oscillation of the mind.

Vikara: Modification or change, generally with reference to the modification of the mind, individually or cosmically.

Vismriti: Oppositise of smritti, (remembrabce) Loss of memory; forgetfulness.

Vistara: Expansion.

Visvasa: Faith.

Viveka: Discrimination between the Real and the unreal, between the Self and the non-Self, between the permanent and the impermanent; right intuitive discrimination; ever-present discrimination between the transient and the permanent.

Vritti: Thought-wave; mental modification; mental whirlpool.

Vyadhi: Disease of the body.

Vyahriti: The sacred syllables, Bhuh, Bhuvah, Svah.

Vyana: One of the five functions of Prana, i.e., circulation of blood; one of the five vital forces that pervades the whole body.

Vyapi: One who pervades.

Yama: The God of Death and dispenser of justice; the first limb of Raja Yoga; restraint.

Yoga: (lit.) Union; abstract meditation or union with the Supreme Being; the name of the philosophy by the sage Patanjali, teaching the process of union of the individual with the Universal Soul: union with God; any course that makes for such union; unruffled state of mind under all conditions. Yoga is mainly of four types: Karma, Bhakti, Raja and Jnana.

Yogi: One who practises Yoga; one who strives earnestly for union with God; an aspirant going through any course of spiritual discipline; one going particularly through the scheduled course of Raja Yoga; a spiritually advanced person with a perfectly unruffled mind under all conditions; a Siddha.

Yuga: See Kalpa. One of the divisions of time. There are four Yugas, known as Krita, Treta, Dvapara and Kali. All the four together are known as a Chaturyuga, the duration of which is twelve thousand divine years, a divine year being equivalent to three hundred and sixty human years. Krita is four times as long as the Kali age; Treta is three times as long; and Dvapara twice as long.